FIGURING OUT THE CHURCH

AIDAN NICHOLS, O.P.

FIGURING OUT THE CHURCH

Her Marks and Her Masters

IGNATIUS PRESS   SAN FRANCISCO

Cover photograph:
Basilica de la Sagrada Familia
Barcelona, Spain
© istockphoto/Roberto A. Sanchez

Cover design by Roxanne Mei Lum

© 2013 by Ignatius Press, San Francisco
All rights reserved
ISBN 978-1-58617-818-5
Library of Congress Control Number 2013941180
Printed in the United States of America ∞

CONTENTS

Preface: Of Marks and Masters 7

PART I
HER MARKS

1. The Unity of the Church 11
2. The Holiness of the Church 33
3. The Catholicity of the Church 57
4. The Apostolicity of the Church 73

PART II
HER MASTERS

5. Henri de Lubac 91
6. Jean Tillard 109
7. Hans Urs von Balthasar 133
8. Charles Journet 153

Conclusion: Should We Love the Church? 177
Select Bibliography 181

PREFACE

OF MARKS AND MASTERS

The most obvious way in which to discuss the Church is by reference to the way in which the Creed describes her: "one, holy, catholic, and apostolic". In a vocabulary which the opening pages of this book will seek to explain, these are her four characteristic signs, notes, or, in the word preferred here, her "marks".

Readers of the work of the French Dominican Cardinal Yves Marie-Jean Congar will realise my debt to that immensely learned historian of ecclesiology, the discipline which studies what, for Christian doctrine, the Church is. It was my good fortune to have profited from several meetings with him at the Couvent Saint-Jacques (and subsequently at Les Invalides) when I was working on a study of a Russian Orthodox ecclesiologist.[1] This emboldened me to accept the invitation of my confrere Father Brian Davies to contribute a little book on Congar's work to the series *Outstanding Christian Thinkers*.[2] As elsewhere,[3] I have followed the main

[1] A. Nichols, O.P., *Theology in the Russian Diaspora: Church, Fathers, Eucharist in Nikolai Afanas'ev, 1893–1966* (Cambridge: Cambridge University Press, 1989).

[2] A. Nichols, O.P., *Yves Congar* (London: Geoffrey Chapman, 1989).

[3] See A. Nichols, O.P., *Come to the Father: An Invitation to Share the Catholic Faith* (London: St Paul's Publications, 2000), pp. 90–106. In my *Epiphany: A Theological Introduction to Catholicism* (Collegeville, Minn.: Liturgical Press, 1996), pp. 234–37, I had followed, rather, the account given in the 1992 *Catechism of the Catholic Church* (nos. 811–65), but while that source is of course more authoritative for Catholic Christians, it is also less lucid, and not so systematic.

lines of his teaching (typical of his middle period) on the marks of the Church. But I have also added enrichments from the dogmatic thought of other authors, whether Scholastic or those under the influence of *la nouvelle théologie*. This description covers the first half of this book. That the concepts used in the ecclesiologies of the Catholic divines often go beyond formal discussion of the four marks suggests the need, however, to "figure out" the Church by scanning more widely the ways in which her "masters" have spoken of her: hence the complement to an account of the "marks of the Church" as provided in the remainder of this modest work.

Once again, I appeal to both the Scholastic tradition and authors influenced by the *ressourcement* movement. I hope that the quartet of masters I have chosen suffices to give readers a breath from a Catholicism that is at once orthodox and generously conceived. These chapters constitute relatively short studies. I cannot possibly hope to do justice to everything they have written relevant to this theme. But there is enough here for my purpose.

I ought to add that, by referring to the Church as "she" (as with "her" marks, "her" masters), it can hardly be overlooked that language about the Church also dwells in symbols and deep metaphors, and not just in concepts and argumentative ratiocination.

In my experience, it is not always easy to love the Church considered as an empirical quantity. But it is, I find, always easy to love her considered as a theological reality. For seen so, she is the Bride of Christ, radiant and crowned with flowers. My conclusion is just about that.

A. NICHOLS, O.P.

Blackfriars, Cambridge
Solemnity of Pentecost, 2012

PART I

HER MARKS

I

THE UNITY OF THE CHURCH

General Introduction

The Creed of Nicaea-Constantinople—the Great Creed, recited for preference whenever there is a confession of faith at Mass—calls the Church "one, holy, catholic, and apostolic". Given that Christian theology is essentially a commentary on the Creed, understood as a summary of Scripture, we should not be surprised to find that much literary production in ecclesiology—the discipline whereby we figure out what the Church is—has taken its structure from these four adjectives.

It is important to notice—not least for the enquiry I have set myself in this small book—that the adjectives in question may be thought of in a number of different ways. The unity, holiness, catholicity, and apostolicity of the Church can be thought of *ontologically*, as four constituent features of the Church's essence. And they can be thought of *epistemologically*, as four signs—the word commonly used is "marks" or "notes"—whereby we can identify the Church (the "true" Church, as people say), i.e., know that the community we are talking about really *is* the Church of the Creed, and, behind the Creed, the Bible.

Moreover, those four adjectives—one, holy, catholic, apostolic—can also be thought of *pedagogically*, as a convenient set of pegs on which to hang whatever it is we wish to say theologically about the Church. Lastly, they can be thought of *eschatologically*, as dimensions of the Church which will receive their full amplitude only in the Age to Come, in that ultimate, consummated existence which belongs to the "heavenly Jerusalem".[1]

These options—ontological, epistemological, pedagogical, eschatological—are in no way mutually exclusive. On the contrary, they cry out (this at any rate is my conviction) for being put together in *synthesis*. If unity, holiness, catholicity, and apostolicity really belong to the Church (the ontological approach), then they will surely manifest themselves in some fashion (the epistemological approach), offering themselves as reference points for whatever else we want to say about the Church (the pedagogical approach), but always with the proviso that any Christian ontology—any account of reality in the light of the Gospel—will need to be open to divine completion from without at the Parousia of the Lord (the eschatological approach).

Preamble to the Mark of Unity

Among the four marks of the Church, the ecumenical Creed —as distinct from the less universally used Old Roman or Apostles' Creed—opts decisively for *unity* as the primordial feature of the Church of God. The Great Creed has already introduced its confession of the Trinitarian life and activity of Father, Son, and Holy Spirit by proclaiming its belief in *one* God, a belief which, significantly, names first the Father

---

[1] As indicated in the Preface, I am indebted at various points in this account of the marks of the Church to Yves Congar, and more especially to his *L'Eglise une, sainte, catholique, et apostolique*, vol. 15 of *Mysterium salutis: Dogmatique de l'histoire du salut* (Paris: Cerf, 1970).

as the fount of the Son and Spirit. I say "significantly" because that fontal position of the Father is crucial to the very
constitution of the Trinity.

These two *credenda*—one Church and one God, named
as Father of Son and Spirit—are not of course unrelated.
There is in some quarters today a tendency to give relative
priority to the inner diversity of the Church rather than to
her unity, to consider her differentiation in the form of multiple local churches, each with (ideally) its own distinctive
life, to be a more interesting theological consideration than
the unity of which the Creed speaks.

Not that people deny outright the unity of the Church,
the need for the Church to correspond in some way to
the mark of oneness. But they are inclined to think of that
unity as something constructed from out of the diversity of
the many local churches of the Catholic Church: an aspect
of their interrelations rather than of their prior productive
ground.

To be theologically consistent, ecclesiologies—or, more
modestly, extended comments on Church life—which run
along these lines probably require a reconstruction of Trinitarian doctrine whereby the Holy Spirit, the Distributor of
multiform gifts, will henceforth be treated as the specific
Trinitarian Person who ought to occupy the foreground of
Christian thinking about God. In that case, the Father, who
in reality is the Source of the Spirit, will be regarded as, in
effect, the presupposition (merely) of the Spirit and thus,
relatively speaking, fade into the background. It is not easy
to get excited about a presupposition! But such a frank reversal of the Trinitarian ordering, which moves essentially
from the Father, who as Father is Father of the Son, to the
Holy Spirit, finds no support (to the regret of advocates of
radically pluralist ecclesiology) in the pattern of the Creed.
Thus any theology that considers itself to consist in obedient

reflection on the Creed as a summary of Scripture, and in that way to be an expression of the Word of God, cannot make room for the reversal. This observation about the theology of the Trinity teaches us, I believe, an important ecclesiological lesson.

It is right and proper to seek theological recognition of the Christian dignity of the local church and a theological validation of legitimate pluralism in thought, worship, and cultural life in the local churches. But this must not be done at the expense of the mark of unity. For the Creed, the Church is not more importantly many than she is one. Indeed, she is not equally importantly many and one. Rather, she is more importantly one than she is many. This is the first conclusion we should draw from the wording of the Creed.

The reason for this—as the back reference from the unity of the Church to the unity of God (one Church, one God) strongly hints—is *the unity of the Father's creating and redeeming plan for the world.* It is because the single Father, in sending his only begotten Son and uniquely spirated Breath into the world, enters upon an all-embracing, overreaching plan of creation and salvation, that there is one and only one Church.

We must now unpack that statement. In the first place, saving an autonomous creation must pass crucially through mankind. In the tenth book of his *Treatise on the Love of God*, Saint Francis de Sales puts it pithily: "Man is the perfection of the universe, the spirit perfects man, love perfects the spirit and charity perfects love. That is why loving God is the aim, the perfection and the excellence of the universe."[2]

---

[2] Cited in E. Stopp, *A Man to Heal Differences: Essays and Talks on St. Francis de Sales* (Philadelphia: Saint Joseph's University Press, 1997), p. 123.

But in the second place, saving an autonomous creation in and via mankind by way of an all-embracing architectonic scheme entails giving very high value not only to the unity of men with God but also to the unity of all men with each other, in relation to God.[3] And so the fathers of the Second Vatican Council could come up with their justly famous formula in the opening paragraph of *Lumen gentium*, the Dogmatic Constitution on the Church: "By her relation to Christ, the Church constitutes a kind of sacrament or sign of intimate union with God and of the unity of all mankind, just as she is an instrument for the realization of such union and unity."[4]

The Manifestation of Unity

Before entering further into the deep waters of the Trinitarian foundation of the Church's unity, let us get our breath for a moment on land. Let us put the question: How does the Church make manifest the unity the Creed ascribes to her? We can look for enlightenment to the Book of Acts, the first ever Church history, which, since it is included in the canon of Scripture, has the further cachet of enjoying the benefits of the charism of inspiration granted to the hagiographs, the authors of the Bible. The Acts of the Apostles

[3] Dom Emmanuel Lanne, abbot of the biritual monastery of Chevetogne, Belgium, wrote of the use of the words "one Church" in the Creeds and early Fathers: "*mia ekklesia* refers back to the unity of God and his plan more than to the notion of union and communion [though] the latter—not directly envisaged—is by no means absent." "L'Eglise une", *Irénikon* 50 (1977): 46–58, here at p. 57.

[4] *Lumen gentium*, no. 1. Walter Kasper (subsequently *praeses* of the Pontifical Council for Christian Unity) spoke of the "grandiose vision of unity" comprised in the "council's fundamental definition of the Church": see W. Kasper, "Die Einheit der Kirche nach dem II. Vatikanischen Konzil", *Catholica* 33 (1979): 262–77.

describes the unity of the first local church, the church of Jerusalem, by saying: "And they held steadfastly to the apostles' teaching and fellowship, to the breaking of the bread and to the prayers" (Acts 2:42). We have here a mention of three elements, and classical Catholic ecclesiology has gone on to identify them as crucial symptoms of the Church's unity.

The sequence in which they are customarily presented runs as follows: hearing the apostles' teaching; participating in the breaking of bread and the prayers; fraternal communion. Applied to the mark of unity, there thus comes about the following scheme. The unity of the Church is a unity in obedient listening to the apostolic preaching, and therefore a unity in faith. It is a unity in the offering of prayers and the Holy Eucharist, and therefore a unity in cult and the celebration of the sacraments. It is a unity in fraternal communion and therefore a unity in social life, with charity as its regulating principle and goal.

These three features are often spoken of—for example, by the French Dominican ecclesiologist Yves Congar—as three types of "bonding", for which the Latin word is *vinculum*.[5] First of all, there is the bonding that gives the Church unity in a common faith expressed in the Symbols (a technical name for the Creeds): the *vinculum symbolicum*, the "symbolic bonding" or (as we should say) "credal bonding". Secondly, there is the bonding whereby the Church all over the world celebrates the same sacraments and recognises an identical worship in her liturgies: the *vinculum liturgicum* or "liturgical bonding". Thirdly, there is the bonding whereby she seeks to mould her members into a common life of charity: the *vinculum sociale*, the "social bonding". Because

---

[5] Congar, *L'Eglise une, sainte, catholique et apostolique*, pp. 13–65.

the latter operates in an ordered way, whereby people in various respects give or receive services and do so within a common discipline over which there preside the pastors of the Church, this particular *vinculum* can also be called the "hierarchical bonding", *vinculum hierarchicum*, and some writers prefer that term for this reason. I note here, just in passing, that in the most ancient view the word *hierarchy* simply means "sacred order" and as such includes all the members of the Church in their ordered coexistence and not just (as modern parlance would have it) the bishops. In any case, each of these three bonds of unity, these *vincula unitatis*, merits our attention.

Credal Bonding

The Church is one because her faith is one. Among the mediaeval Scholastics, probably the single most common brief formula for speaking of the Church was *congregatio fidelium*, the "assembly of those who have faith". For the Schoolmen, the word *congregatio* was more or less interchangeable with any of a number of terms (*societas*, "society"; *corpus*, "body"; *collectio*, "collection"; *coetus*, "group") for a set of people who are one by having as their common goal some shared principle for living and acting.[6] In the ecclesiological context, then, to add to the term *congregatio* the specifying term *fidelium* is to make the point that in the Church this unifying principle is faith itself. Receiving by obedient attention the apostolic teaching is the very first thing people will have in common in the Church so as to be made there into a unity.

[6] Ibid., pp. 22–23.

Can we sum that up by saying that those who belong to the Church hold the same propositions to be true? Certainly, that claim belongs properly to the *vinculum symbolicum*, and yet the latter goes beyond the issue of propositions. The propositions—drawn typically from the articles of the Creed—always have a wider context in the act of faith by which we make the saving disclosure of the self-revealing God our own. Faith, as Congar points out in discussing this topic, is a welcoming openness to the initiative of God whereby we take our stand on God's own veracity and faithfulness—shown above all in his incarnate Son, the fulfillment of the promises to Israel, and in this way enter into God's everlasting New Covenant.[7] However—and here is where the propositions come into play—such reception of God's personal Word cannot be conceived anti-doctrinally or even non-doctrinally. It is (literally!) unthinkable without an intellectual engagement on our part. It involves a conscious reception of fresh understanding, the acceptance of novel certitudes about the purpose of existence and its destiny. By faith, then, the members of the Church believe in the same realities, as communicated by the witness of the Scriptures and the oral teaching of the apostles, transmitted through the Church's mission of teaching, which is the prolongation of the apostles' own.

Believing in the same realities is not, then, a massive coincidence befalling a lot of individuals at the same time. The content of divine revelation is not given individually, to each person, in the privacy of his conscience. Rather, it is given publicly to a corporate subject, the apostolic community, in the latter's relation to its predecessor community, Israel. And so the way a single faith unites the Church's members

[7] Ibid., p. 23.

cannot satisfactorily be described in interior terms alone. It is not simply a consequence of each member receiving the same inner grace. Revelation has mediators who were or are publicly available: prophets, apostles, coworkers of the apostles, and, last of all in salvation-historical time, the subsequent bearers of the magisterial, or teaching, authority instituted by Christ—those who hold office in the Church by apostolic succession. True, these human mediations of faith are never the object of faith, for the object of faith is the Word of God alone. And yet the authority of their deliverances is so bound up with the communication of the divine Word that they possess a normative value for the community's credal belief.[8] Saint Paul wrote to the Church at Corinth: "I appeal to you, brethren, by the name of our Lord Jesus Christ, that all of you agree and that there be no dissensions among you, but that you be united in the same mind and the same judgment" (1 Cor 1:10). Concretely, that is only possible if the authentic content of revelation is accessible in the form of a corporate rule of faith in the Church.

We can compare that claim with the position of Saint Thomas. What, for Thomas, a person adheres to in the act of believing is never anything less than God himself as *Prima Veritas*, the "First Truth", and yet, at the same time (as Thomas writes in his treatise on faith in the *Summa theologiae*), that First Truth is "proposed to us in the Scriptures according to the teaching of the Church which enjoys their right understanding."[9] Thus, for instance, the faith of a Catholic Christian in the divinity of Christ does not have its rule—its criterion—*simply* in the Scriptures, for the

---

[8] An always reliable guide to this subject is A. Dulles, S.J., *Magisterium: Teacher and Guardian of the Faith* (Naples, Fl.: Sapientia Press, 2007).

[9] Thomas Aquinas, *Summa theologiae* IIa. IIae., q. 5, a. 3, corpus and ad ii.

Scriptures alone did not prevent Arius of Alexandria from teaching that the Son is a created intermediary. Catholic faith in the Son's Godhood has its rule also in an act of the Church's extraordinary magisterium, the dogma of the *homoousion* proclaimed at Nicaea I (325), and the continuing profession of faith in the Son of God that we find in the Church's Liturgy—and the Liturgy might well be considered the principal expression of the Church's ordinary magisterium, the place where the great majority of the faithful receive their knowledge of the mysteries of revelation. *Dogma* and the *Liturgy*, once their deliverances are internalised with the help of interior grace, unite believers at the highest level by adjusting their outlook to that of the Word incarnate in his human fullness. They enable believers to participate in the mind of Christ—his human consciousness of the triune God to whom his humanity was inseparably but unconfusedly united—and his awareness, in his own mission and that of the Spirit who indwelt him, of the Father's saving plan: in brief, what he was, and what he was about.

Liturgical Bonding

Mention of the Liturgy brings us by a natural progression to the second manifestation of the Church's unity, the *vinculum liturgicum*, which is the bonding together of the Church as one by means of cultic and (especially) sacramental signs. How should we understand this?

Of itself, faith places us in a doxological—and therefore a worshipful—attitude towards God. The knowledge that faith brings is not, evidently, of an academic kind. It is knowledge of the love for us of the One who is Alpha and Omega, our absolute Source and unconditional End. Expressed outwardly, faith naturally takes the form, then, of cult, and cult of its nature has a social character. A self-devised form of worship, carried out in privacy, would in any conceivable human context be an extremely odd thing. Every social manifestation of cult is, for any worshipping group, a principle of unity. This unity will be found not only in deploying the same symbols and gestures but also in forming a common awareness and sensibility that is prompted by the symbols and gestures concerned and finds expression in them.

The chief component of Christian worship is the Liturgy of the sacraments, in which these principles are embodied. Embodied and also (we can say) transcended, surpassed, gone beyond.

In the sacraments, we are dealing not merely with a social principle of unity, as in a cult where social anthropologists could study its functioning. Nor are we just dealing with some natural unity attaching to the human intention that underlies (as social psychologists might wish to assert) participation in such cultic activity at large. Rather, in sacramental practice we have a unique underlying intention, the grace-enabled intention of ecclesial faith whose term is God himself. In the sacraments, the saving acts put in place in historical time by the Word incarnate make available the grace of the Father via bodily actions, and they do so through the medium of the Holy Spirit, by whose invocation (whether tacit or explicit) all sacramental acts come to be. For ecclesiology, this will mean that the Church's members, in receiving the same sacraments, are joined to each other by sharing in the supernatural life that flows from these embodied continuations of the work of Christ.

In the first place, and by way of basic foundation, the faithful are united by the royal priesthood bestowed on them in

Holy Baptism, whereby they are sacramentally initiated into the Covenant the Suffering Servant inaugurated in the River Jordan and subsequently realised in his own Person by his Passion, through which he rose to endless life (and equally endless *giving* of life). Holy Baptism is the primary sacramental bond of our unity in Christ.

In the second place, and by way of supreme importance, the union of the faithful in the same sacraments refers to the mystery of the Holy Eucharist, the communion-sacrifice that renews Christ's Passover from death to life every time it is celebrated and binds us more closely together in the New Covenant made in his Blood. That is why Tradition calls the Eucharist *sacramentum unitatis*: the "sacrament of unity".

It is because the divine life was supremely outpoured from Calvary, where each Trinitarian Person contributed in his own way to the act of reconciliation reuniting the world to God—the Father willing and receiving the Sacrifice, the Son executing it, the Spirit communicating its effect—that the Mass has a fuller capacity than any other liturgical sign —even Baptism—to unite men to God and to each other in God. The unity of the Church in charity—which means *in God*—is the final point of the Eucharist, what classical Latin theology has called its *res*: literally, its "thing", what the Mass is ultimately all about.

The sacramental body of Christ assimilates the Church's communicant members to Christ's personal Body as offered, immolated, raised, and glorified. And in this way the sacramental Body ceaselessly generates his Mystical Body, the Church herself. It sustains her unity, and where the cooperation of human freedom is forthcoming, it deepens it as well.

The Eucharist, then, is not the sacrament of just any kind of bonding—*bonhomie*, for example, or the unity of the cultural, ethnic, or social category of people who may be celebrating it in some given situation. Instead, the Eucharist is specifically the sacrament of *paschal charity*—it flows from the total self-gift of Jesus to the Father in his life-giving death for all men. Thus the charity it produces can only be that love which gives itself to God and all men inseparably—a love that is the heart of the Church when she is considered as the sign and instrument of union with God and unity among people en route to the heavenly Jerusalem.

Owing to some contemporary abuses that, regrettably, have crept into Church life here and there, it is worth saying at this point that to instrumentalise the sacrament of such unity for any lesser cause—ideological, political, ethnic, or whatever—can only frustrate the nature of the Holy Eucharist as the *vinculum liturgicum* par excellence of the Church. In the second part of this book, we shall see how an important contribution to Catholic ecclesiology of twentieth-century writers has been to take further the Eucharistic dimension of the *vinculum liturgicum* under the name of "Eucharistic ecclesiology". That should not be thought of as the whole of ecclesiology (another modern mistake), but it is, nevertheless, one of ecclesiology's most important themes. And of course it underlines the need to celebrate the Mass in a way that is worthy of the Catholic tradition —and hence of this supreme sacrament.

Social Bonding

Thought of the community of charity brings us to the third kind of bonding whereby the Church's unity is made manifest, and that is the *vinculum sociale*. The nature of the Church's social unity differs fundamentally from that of any other human grouping. Of course, those who belong to the Church also belong to other natural human groupings, such as families, circles of friends, neighbourhoods, professional or recreational associations, civic communities, and nation states. Consequently, the theologically unique nature of their relations with others *specifically as Catholic Christians* may not always be clear to them. The natural unities I have mentioned complicate the picture, though they are also capable of being taken up into the specific social unity that characterises the Church.

The charity-love that typifies the Church as such does not unify after the manner of other socially unifying principles. It cannot since, unlike them, it is not humanly constructed. Not a humanly originated benevolence, it unifies the Church by virtue of the distinctive way it originates in the Holy Spirit, to whom in the Godhead love is especially attributed, owing to the Spirit's Trinitarian position as the One who is personally the uncreated Love binding together the Father and the Son. The charity-love whereby the Holy Spirit bonds the faithful together brings about a different kind of unity from those known elsewhere because charity works by making the Church's members *sharers in the unity of the Holy Trinity itself.*

So whatever the providential role of the Holy Spirit may be in the formation of other social unities, his functioning in the building up of the Body of Christ is *sui generis.*

In its social manifestation, ecclesial charity can be investigated under two rubrics. And these are charity as service and charity as communion.[10] In the perspective of charity as *service*, the Church's unity may be described as a network of mutually assisting agencies at all levels. These run from the pope articulating doctrine in the worldwide Church to an

---

[10] Congar, *L'Eglise, une, sainte, catholique et apostolique*, pp. 41–45.

ordinary parishioner going to visit another because the latter is sick. Saint Thomas speaks of the social unity of the Church as the "reciprocal sub-ministration" (*mutua subministratio*) of a vast range of services that we can do each other.[11] This concept integrates several themes in the New Testament Letters—notably, *diakonia*, service of ministry; *charismata*, gifts, whether unspectacular or amazing; and *oikodomê*, the building of the Church's house. Charity as service is about meeting the needs of others in the Church.

There is also, however, charity as *communion*, which is concerned not with doing anything remotely useful but simply enjoying coexistence with others. As principle of the Church's social unity, the Holy Spirit renders the faithful, both living and departed, supernaturally open to one another in the communion of saints. In an activist world, it is easy to forget that enjoying being with others is the highest form of union with them. But true friends are aware of it. To echo Saint Augustine, they will know what I mean. Here one might mention the winning portrait of the Church as a holding together of unity and freedom in mutual love (*sobornost*) painted by the nineteenth-century Russian ecclesiologist Alexei Khomiakov, which influenced the young Congar.[12]

That said, the communion of the faithful, one with another, has a dimension of public interaction and thus itself needs to be rightly ordered. Here we recall that the *vinculum sociale* can also be termed a *vinculum hierarchicum* (something greatly underestimated by Khomiakov but properly appreciated by Congar). Stemming from the apostles, responsibility

---

[11] Thomas Aquinas, *Summa theologiae* IIa. IIae., q. 183, a. 3, corpus.

[12] J. Famerée, "Orthodox Influence on the Roman Catholic Theologian Yves Congar, O.P.: A Sketch", *Saint Vladimir's Theological Quarterly* 39 (1995): 409–16.

for overseeing the peace of the Church devolves on the Church's pastors, which means in the first place the pope and bishops. They should so exercise their authority as to ensure, so far as is possible, the spiritual communion of the faithful in charity and the smooth operation of the mutual services that charity prompts. The same charity that animates the inner communion of the faithful should also inspire the conduct of their organised life.

The Origin of the Church's Unity in the Triune God

So much for the threefold bond in which the unity of the Church becomes manifest. It is unity in the same faith, in the same sacraments, and in a common life under the guidance of the same pastors. Can we now say more about the origination of that unity in the life of the triune God?

I have already suggested that an account of the unity that follows the cue of the Creed must take care not to invert the Trinitarian ordering by leaving the Father till last as a mere presupposition of the work of the Spirit of the Son. And yet, if we can believe historians of the Creeds, the concluding articles of the Creed, which concern the Church, salvation, and the Last Things, were, in the early history of the text, governed by the preliminary reference to the Holy Spirit.[13] It would not, therefore, compromise the intention of the Creed's makers were we to paraphrase the article on the Church: "We believe in the Holy Spirit, . . . who unifies the Church, rendering her holy, catholic, and apostolic." An ecclesiology faithful to the Creed must enjoy close links

[13] J. N. D. Kelly, *Early Christian Creeds* (London: Longmans, Green, & Co., 1950), pp. 155–66.

with pneumatology—a theology of the Holy Spirit—not least in this matter of the *unity* of the Church.

Helpful here is the work of the Paderborn theologian Heribert Mühlen, who during the Second Vatican Council explored the Church as "the mystery of the identity of the Holy Spirit in Christ and in Christians: one Person in many persons". Mühlen points out that common usage—every Catholic should know this from any catechism—contains two concise doctrinal formulae when speaking of God in Christ. In regard to the Trinity, God is "three Persons in one nature"; in regard to Christology, Christ is "one Person in two natures". Mühlen thinks we might well complete that duet of maxims by a third, which would provide a pneumatological and ecclesiological counterpart to the other two: the Holy Spirit is "one Person in many persons, namely, in Christ and ourselves".[14] By this means, and without seeking in any sense to marginalise the reference of the Church to Christ, whose Body and Bride she is, the scattered allusions of the New Testament and the subsequent monuments of Tradition to the Holy Spirit as the unifying principle of the Church may be dogmatically clarified.

What Mühlen proposes is, in effect, this: not only the *vinculum sociale* but also the *vinculum symbolicum* and the *vinculum liturgicum*—everything, then, that holds the Church together —must be understood in the context of a deeper and more comprehensive bond, the *vinculum pneumaticum* or "pneumatic bonding" whereby the Holy Spirit unites Christ and ourselves in the one Church of the divine-human Mediator, who is our blessed Saviour. As he writes: "Christ binds us

---

[14] Strictly speaking, in English it would be best to lay out the word *persons* there as "Person/persons" because the phrase "Christ and ourselves" includes, of course, one single divine Person, with an uppercase *P*, as well as a vast multiplicity of human persons, with a lowercase *p*.

to himself and binds himself to us through the sending of the Holy Spirit, so that the Spirit, while binding himself to us and us with himself, brings about our union with Christ. And therefore he is the *vinculum*, the bond of unity; he himself, then, is the numerically one Person in Christ and us."[15] In the economy of salvation, the Spirit performs the same task as he does in the Holy Trinity: namely, to be the nexus of unity, not this time between the Father and the Son, but between the Son according to his humanity and ourselves.

In the Trinity, the Hypostasis of the Son is constituted by "filiation": the Son's relation of "passive generation" to the Father. But a full description of the second divine Hypostasis is not possible (at least so Catholics say, the Orthodox diverge here) without also mentioning the Son's "active spiration" with the Father of the Holy Spirit, the third divine Person. Now in the moment of the Incarnation, the Father, never without his Son, bestows that Spirit on the humanity of Christ. The Church, for Mühlen, is the continuation of this act of bestowal, which the Gospel according to Saint Luke locates primordially at the Annunciation episode, the Gospel tradition at large associates in particular with the Baptism in the Jordan, and the Letters of Saint Paul link in climactic form with the Resurrection of the Crucified. Thanks to this accumulating series of mysterial events —Annunciation, Baptism, Resurrection of the Crucified— the Holy Spirit is now supremely the Spirit of Christ. As the Gospel according to Saint John puts it, "not by measure" does Jesus have the Spirit (Jn 3:34). On the contrary, Jesus has the Spirit in unmeasurable—incomparable—fashion because he is the very principle of the Spirit's economic mani-

[15] H. Mühlen, *Una mystica Persona: Die Kirche als das Mysterium der Identität des Heiligen Geistes in Christus und den Christen; eine Person in vielen Personen*, 2nd ed. (Paderborn: Aschendorf, 1967), p. 18.

festation.[16] In ourselves, contrastingly, the presence of the Spirit is very definitely "measured", that is, distinctly limited. Nevertheless, Saint Augustine, who certainly affirmed a "distance of majesty" between Christ and us, could still describe Christ's bonding to the Church as so intimate that it makes of Christ and the Church *una quaedam persona*, "as it were one person".[17] And it is the peculiar excellence of Mühlen that he gives a good explanation of how this can be.

The unity of this *persona* will not of course be the hypostatic unity whereby the Word and the humanity the Word assumed in Mary's womb are one Person. The Church's members are not one through hypostatic union with Christ. Rather, the unity of the *una quaedam persona* comes about through the mediation of the Holy Spirit, who is himself one and the same in Christ and ourselves. Thus the unity of the Church in Christ is not, after all (*pace* my opening remarks on this note of the Creed), *simply* the result of the Father's predisposing plan. The Father's predisposing plan is to render a world created and saved a unity in the human species *precisely by sending the Holy Spirit to be one single Person in the Word incarnate and ourselves.* We—Christ and each other in the Church—form *una mystica persona,* "one mystical person".

That phrase, originally (so it would seem) a coining by Saint Thomas, was introduced into modern Catholic theology by the Dutch Jesuit Sebastian Tromp, the principal author of Pius XII's encyclical on the nature of the Church, *Mystici corporis Christi.*[18] Mühlen's effort is in clear continuity

[16] Ibid.

[17] Augustine, *Ennaration on Psalm 30*, II. 4.

[18] Thomas Aquinas, *Summa theologiae* IIIa, q. 9, a. 4, ad i. The formula (with the adjective following the noun) recurs in very different writings of Thomas,

with the Pian letter owing to their similarity of aim. Pius XII was seeking to refute both a naturalism that treated the Church as though she were merely a social organisation and a pseudo-mysticism that treated her as literally one person with Christ in the "pan-Christism" beloved of some inter-War German Catholic ecclesiologists, which has been revived today in a new form by the Greek Orthodox theologian Bishop John Zizioulas.[19] (There will be something much more favourable to say about Bishop Zizioulas' contribution when we come to consider the fourth note, the apostolicity of the Church.)

Mühlen sought to meet the doctrinal demands set by Pope Pius' letter through applying to the Church of the New Testament a version of the idea of corporate personality as found in the Old.[20] Just as in the Old Testament an ancestor—Adam, say, or Abraham—could be said to be "in" his descendants and they "in" him, so, likewise, thanks to the outpouring of the Spirit on the basis of the saving work of the Son, Christ can be "in" us and we "in" him in the communion of the Church. Commenting on this saying of Saint Paul, "[H]e who joins himself to a prostitute becomes one body with her. . . . But he who is united to the Lord becomes one spirit with him" (1 Cor 6:17), the exegete Rudolf Schnackenburg wrote:

---

from the *Disputed Questions on Truth* to his commentary on St. Paul's Letter to the Colossians: see for other examples, Mühlen, *Una mystica Persona*, pp. 40–44.

[19] "[T]he Mystery of Christ is in essence nothing other than the Mystery of the Church." J. Zizioulas, "The Mystery of the Church in Orthodox Tradition", *One in Christ* 24 (1988): 294–303; here at p. 303. This programmatic essay makes much of the corporate personality idea.

[20] H. Wheeler-Robinson, *Corporate Personality in Ancient Israel* (Philadelphia: Fortress, 1964).

[This] expression draws attention to what is dissimilar within this analogy: the relationship with Christ despite the closest imaginable union is nevertheless of a different kind, a community which comes about [through] and is characterized by the Spirit. For the Body of Christ . . . , the *pneuma* which proceeds from the Lord is the principle of unity . . . ; it links the baptized with Christ as well as with one another.[21]

Essentially, then, Heribert Mühlen's work enables us to see how, when we call Christ the Head of the Mystical Body and the Church the members of that Body and take the two together to constitute "one mystical person", we are *implicitly appealing to the work of the Holy Spirit* in Christ and ourselves.

So far in this discussion of unity and multiplicity in the Church, we have been speaking of the many individual persons who compose the Church. Something more needs to be said, however, about another type of multiplicity—the many local churches that also, on a different level, "compose" her. But I shall deal with that under the third of the Church's marks, that of catholicity.

---

[21] R. Schnackenburg, *The Church in the New Testament* (Freiburg and London: Herder & Herder, 1965), p. 169.

2

THE HOLINESS OF THE CHURCH

Introduction

The affirmation of the Creed of Nicaea-Constantinople that the Church is holy, *Credo in . . . sanctam . . . Ecclesiam*, means that belief in the holiness of the Church is not just a pious opinion. Far less is it a sentimental illusion. Rather, it is a certitude of faith. The received text of the Apostles' Creed agrees: *Credo . . . sanctam Ecclesiam*, "I believe that the Church is holy",[1] that the Holy Spirit (in Saint Thomas' paraphrase) "sanctifies the Church".[2] True, the expression "holy Church", beloved of earlier generations (as in Newman's hymnic lines from *The Dream of Gerontius*: "And I hold in veneration, / For the love of Him alone, / *Holy Church* as His creation"),[3] is not actually found in Scripture. But Catholic theology has long regarded it as an implication of the Letter to the Ephesians: "Christ loved the Church and gave himself up for her, that he might sanctify her, having cleansed her by the washing of water with the word, that he might present the Church to himself in splendour, without

[1] P. O'Callaghan, "The Holiness of the Church in Early Christian Creeds", *Irish Theological Quarterly* 54 (1988): 59–65.

[2] Thomas Aquinas, *Summa theologiae* IIa. IIae., q. 1, a. 9, ad v.

[3] John Henry Newman, *Newman: Prose and Poetry*, ed. G. Tillotson (London: Rupert Hart-Davis, 1957), pp. 814–15.

spot or wrinkle or any such thing, that she might be holy and without blemish" (Eph 5:25b–27). At the late patristic and mediaeval councils, the phrase *sancta Ecclesia* became in fact a received formula for referring to the Church, in the wake of the Creed's explicit formulation of the Bible's tacit statement of the Church's essential holiness.

The Holiness of the Church Seen Apologetically

In the opening chapter, I said that speaking of the Church as one and holy, as also catholic and apostolic, need not be done only in an ontological fashion, as a way of evoking (that is) the Church's deep-down nature. These expressions—naming the marks of the Church—can also function (*inter alia*) epistemologically, as ways of identifying the true Church from among various societies at work in history. This is how the fathers of the First Vatican Council (1869–1870) were thinking when they declared the Church's holiness a "motive of credibility"—a reason for believing in Christian revelation in its Catholic form. By her outstanding holiness, they wrote, and "inexhaustible fecundity in all good", the Church gives witness to her divine mandate.[4]

The force of this claim can be brought out by distinguishing, as many theologians in the later Scholastic tradition do, between *positive* marks of the Church and *negative* ones. As is the way of Scholastic Latin, terms do not necessarily mean what they might seem to mean when transposed directly into English. And this is the case here. A "negative mark" of the Church is not, as perhaps we would think, the sort of judgment likely to be made on the Catholic Church by a hostile observer: Ms. Polly Toynbee, say, writing in the *Guardian*

---

[4] *Dei Filius*, no. 3.

newspaper. What Neo-Scholastics mean by a "negative mark" is a characteristic of the Church—for example, faith in the divinity of Christ or stewardship of sacraments—that can be found simultaneously in a number of confessional bodies and which is, therefore, insufficient to allow us positively to recognise the Church of Christ in any one ecclesial society on earth. Such marks can be said to take us forward in identifying the Church "negatively" inasmuch as their absence will lead one to strike off the list certain contenders. Thus the Salvation Army or the Society of Friends cannot be the Church of Christ, admirable in certain respects though they are, because they lack one or more of these indicators (sacraments, or faith in Christ's divinity).

For post-Tridentine Scholastic thought, a positive mark of the Church must be more than this. As a visible mark of the Church's legitimacy, it must be the exclusive attribute of some one particular body. There can indeed be *kinds* of unity and holiness, as of catholicity and apostolicity, found in other Christian bodies, but on this epistemological understanding of the four marks of the Church, they are not quite the same *sort* of unity and holiness, catholicity and apostolicity, as those that belong to the *vera Ecclesia*, "the true Church", taken as such. That is a relevant distinction when we are approaching the topic of the Church's holiness epistemologically—as an index for picking out from a number of candidates that Church in which, to use the language of the Second Vatican Council (1962–1965), the mystical Church–Body of Christ "subsists".[5]

How, then, has classical apologetics treated the mark of holiness as a way of singling out the (Roman) Catholic Church in particular as the actual referent of this statement of the

---

[5] *Lumen gentium*, no. 8.

Creed? In this context, so it is said, in order to conform to the Creed's account, the Church must be both holy in her principles and holy in her members.[6] Let us take these two in turn.

First, the Church must be holy "in her principles". What does this mean? So as to be *sancta Ecclesia*, the Church must be by her principles the instrument of the sanctification of her members, in line with the fact that Christ came to found as first fruits of the divine Kingdom a new Israel that would unite men to God, on earth by grace, in heaven by glory, since for this end—union with God—sanctification is inevitably required. It is a conviction of the entire biblical revelation that whatever is not holy cannot endure in God's sight. Suitable sanctifying principles are to be found in the Church's sacraments, her Scriptures, her doctrines, the discipline of her common life, in the evangelical counsels of poverty, chastity, and obedience, and the ethos these hold out to all who practice charity by loving God and their neighbour.

Now in order to be the wherewithal of "holy Church" these sanctifying principles must coexist in their total ensemble. It is not enough, for instance, to have the sacraments without the Scriptures, or vice versa. Moreover, these principles must function in such a way as to assure their real end, the holiness of men, and for this they must in practice be entrusted to a leadership (call it a "ministry" or a "magisterium") that knows how to make use for them for the purposes of human salvation. Sanctifying principles need to be properly operative, or they are next to useless. Thus, for example, possession of the Scriptures is not in itself the re-

---

[6] A. Michel, "La sainteté, note de l'Eglise", in *Dictionnaire de théologie catholique*, vol. 14, fasc. 1 (Paris: Letouzey & Ané, 1939), cols. 847–65.

ceipt of a gift of a sanctifying principle for one's life if one knows how to read the Scriptures only after the manner of nineteenth-century Source Critics or 1960s' Structuralists.[7] One must know how to read the Scriptures in the same Spirit in which they were written if one is to find them, in the words of Second Timothy, "profitable for teaching, for reproof, for correction, and for training in righteousness, that the man of God may be complete, equipped for every good work" (2 Tim 3:16b–17). It is the responsibility of the apostolic ministry in the Church to see to it that the holiness of these operative principles, themselves stemming from God in Christ, passes with full effect into the members of the Church. The question then arises (and it is an open one): Do other ecclesial bodies (apart from the Catholic Church) have such a ministry which can bring about this result?

Secondly, after holiness of the Church's principles, what about the holiness of the Church's members, that further constituent of the general idea of ecclesial holiness as such? The New Testament Letters are full of references to the holiness of life expected of the Church's members. For Ephesians, the members of the Church are built into a holy temple in the Lord as a dwelling place for God in the Spirit. For the Johannine Letters, they stand in a relation to God of adoptive filiation (sonship) and thus, as the Letter to the Hebrews and the Second Letter of Peter agree, participate in the holiness of God himself. Such participated holiness is shown not only by the avoidance of evil but also, and here the First Letter of Saint John and numerous Pauline texts would agree, by an abundance of spiritual fruit in a life focussed on love of God and neighbour, the primary precepts of the New Law.

---

[7] I. de la Potterie, "Reading Holy Scripture 'in the Spirit': Is the Patristic Way of Reading the Bible Still Possible Today?" *Communio* 4 (1986): 308–25.

All this is summed up in Saint Paul's Letter to Titus: "Jesus Christ . . . gave himself for us to redeem us from all iniquity and to purify for himself a people of his own who are zealous for good deeds" (Titus 2:14).

In the New Testament, such practical holiness on the part of the Church's members has an evidential value, pertinent, obviously enough, to an epistemological view of the mark of holiness. According to the Synoptic tradition, Jesus had taught that a good tree may be told by the quality of the fruit it bears. That is echoed by Saint Paul when in the Letter to the Galatians he draws a contrast between manifest works of the flesh, which mark out those who do them as excluded from the Kingdom, and the fruits of the Spirit, which single out those who belong to Christ.

Does all this imply that holiness must be patently realised in each and every member of the Church? Apparently not. Jesus spoke of the scandals that would come in the community of his disciples: good wheat and good-for-nothing tares would grow beside each other until the end of the age. We can reconcile these two sets of prima facie conflicting biblical data by saying that in *vera Ecclesia* there must be enough evangelically holy men and women for a humanly inexplicable holiness to appear there as the proper effect of the sanctifying principles bestowed by Christ on his people. And that is, incidentally, the main argument for the truth of Christianity used by Saint Augustine in the opening sections of his treatise *On the True Religion*.[8]

Before grappling with the question of whether we can ascribe the realisation of this mark of holiness—holiness of principles, holiness of members—to the (Roman) Catholic Church in particular, it may be helpful to introduce some

---

[8] Augustine, *De vera religione*, 1–4.

simple distinctions of which the later Scholastic tradition makes use. The distinctions in question yield up concepts which can be described as internal to the idea of personal holiness.

Such Scholastics distinguish "common holiness" from "more perfect holiness" and that again from "heroic sanctity".[9] *Common holiness* denotes the graced condition which anyone who even minimally corresponds with the precepts of Christ and the Church will embody. There are Christian virtues that, even when lived out only in a mediocre fashion, nonetheless give a Christian culture a certain sign-value when compared with its pagan counterparts—thanks to the impact, diffused though it is, of supernatural life in a fallen world.

There can thus be an index of transcendence in common holiness (the patchily realised ethical qualities of a Christian culture), even if this can hardly function as a *positive* mark —a principle of clear discernment—when comparing one Christian civilisation with another. By what concrete criteria might, say, a Catholic civilisation be judged more obviously graced than an Orthodox, Lutheran, or Anglican civilisation in its moral culture, its art, music, literature? That can scarcely be called an easy question to answer, though the early nineteenth-century French Romantic apologist François-René de Chateaubriand attempted something approximately like it in his *Génie du Christianisme*.[10]

Next, in terms of these Scholastic, or Neo-Scholastic, distinctions comes *more perfect holiness*—School-talk for the life of the evangelical counsels, a form of following Christ through the renunciation of possessions and family and the

[9] Michel, "La sainteté, note de l'Eglise", cols. 851–53.
[10] F. R. de Chateaubriand, *Le Génie du Christianisme, ou beautés de la religion chrétienne* (Paris: Migneret, 1802).

acceptance of voluntary submission to an ascetic rule, guarded by a superior, all in the interest of growth in the perfect love of God and neighbour. Such a life, so it is suggested, exceeds the bounds of natural inclinations and possibilities, and ought to count as a manifestation of ecclesial holiness in the Church's members.

Finally, *heroic sanctity* is the supreme epiphany of holiness in the Church's members (and indirectly, of the holiness of her principles as well). It is the perfect imitation of Christ in maximal self-giving to God, expressed most strikingly perhaps in the love of enemies and the readiness for martyrdom. That of course is the quality of holiness sought out in enquiries leading to beatification and canonisation of "servants of God".

"Favourable Prejudices"

But we have yet to apply these observations to the issue of how the many different *de facto* church bodies stand vis-à-vis the *una sancta* Church of the Creed. Albin Michel, writing in the *Dictionnaire de théologie catholique*, the most elaborate reference work produced by a predominantly Neo-Scholastic theological culture, argues that a holiness capable of constituting a legitimising mark of the Church is present among those in communion with the Roman See but absent from the rest.[11]

Michel organises his case under the two headings we have already encountered—holiness of principles, holiness of members. But he prefaces his material by a preliminary consideration of what he calls "favourable prejudices": prior considerations which might dispose us towards a sympa-

[11] Michel, "La sainteté, note de l'Eglise", cols. 854–70.

thetic reading of the evidence, or the arguments, he intends to present.

These "favourable prejudices" turn out to be twofold. First, Michael cites the way the Catholic Church is of all Christian bodies the most pilloried and satirised, attacked and even persecuted. That, he thinks, should alert us, given certain New Testament texts on the topic of the opposition disciples will arouse. The travails of the Catholic Church in the wider public forum should wake us up to the possibility that we are dealing here with "the true and unique depositary of the treasures of holiness on which human beings must draw to reach their salvation".[12] In his *Essay on the Development of Christian Doctrine*, Blessed John Henry Newman put forward a similar argument for the case that, despite appearances, the Church of Rome *is* the Church of the early centuries,[13] though Michel's formulation is drawn not so much from Newman as from the early nineteenth-century political theologian Joseph de Maistre. Whatever ideological position people are coming from, writes Michel, "all know where they must strike".[14]

Michel's second antecedent consideration concerns the phenomenon of inter-confessional conversion. Generally speaking, Michel claims, conversions to Catholicism from either Protestantism or Orthodoxy are motivated by sheer religious desire, whereas conversions that move in the reverse direction tend to include a certain admixture of human respect: concern for social respectability, ethnic solidarity, political acceptability. (I have to say that, had Michel lived to the end of the twentieth century, he would have

[12] Ibid., col. 854.
[13] J. H. Newman, *An Essay on the Development of Christian Doctrine: The Edition of 1845* (Harmondsworth: Penguin, 1974), pp. 241–42.
[14] Michel, "La sainteté, note de l'Eglise", col. 854.

some difficulty in explaining on this basis the conversion to Eastern Orthodoxy of many American Evangelicals, and indeed a number of Latin Catholics in Western Europe and North America.) That issue is relevant to the question of ecclesial holiness because what is at stake in the matter of such conversions is the *quality* of the conversions involved. That Church which embodies the *sancta Ecclesia* of the Creed can be expected to draw people in a different way than do others—though here allowance has to be made for contingent factors such as (in the current period) the disorienting effect of such unexpected episodes as a not entirely successful reform Council.

The Case for Rome: Sanctifying Principles

So much for the antecedent favourable considerations. What, then, of the material to which such considerations are expected to dispose us? Where the ecclesial holiness of the sanctifying *principles* in the Church is concerned, Michel sees some specifically Catholic doctrines as maximising the potential of sanctifying principles that in themselves are also to be found in, say, the churches of the Orthodox East. Examples would include the teaching of the Second Council of Lyons (1274) that the communion of saints includes souls in Purgatory with the consequent possibility of offering suffrages to assist the progress of the departed towards the vision of God. Another instance is found in the interrelated Tridentine doctrines of justification by faith-working-through-charity and of grace appropriated through freedom as supernatural merit. These specifically Catholic dogmatic formulations do seem to be especially encouraging for movement towards sanctification (whether one's own or that of others). Here we must recall how only that Church which, in regard to the principles that make for holiness, *exercises them in a fully integrated manner* can be said to possess those principles in the sense implied by the *sancta Ecclesia* clause of the Creed.

Moreover, still on sanctity of principles, the way Catholic Christianity proposes a specific discipline of life—ethical, spiritual, devotional (one might think here of the third and fourth books of the 1992 *Catechism of the Catholic Church*)— permits the faithful to draw the maximum benefit from the means of grace. Again, Michel has already asserted, reasonably enough, that only the Church whose ministry or magisterium knows how to apply effectively the principles making for holiness corresponds to the *sancta Ecclesia*.

Finally, the public institutional regulation of the impulse to live out the evangelical counsels by the canonical recognition of religious orders (a peculiarity of Catholicism, albeit imitated by Anglo-Catholics) is, Michel finds, a means to the consolidation of that same impulse to a "more perfect holiness" than is "common holiness". And this phenomenon of religious orders is found—on any significant scale—only in the Catholic Church. The Anglican Communion has in the last two hundred years a noble tradition of monastic and religious life, but it is both numerically small and confined almost exclusively to the Anglo-Catholic wing of the Church of England (and some other provinces).

I think it should be said, however, that while the religious orders, for both men and women, are certainly a striking element in the overall make-up of the Catholic Church, that Church as a whole does not have so strongly marked a monastic ethos as does Byzantine Orthodoxy—specifically, surely, owing to the requirement that the members of the episcopate in the Orthodox churches be themselves monastics. That is so even if, in the Orthodox context, the consecrated life is not set at the service of the total communion of the Church in *so many different ways* as we find in the churches in peace and unity with the See of Rome. I shall return to this below.

The Case for Rome:
The Holiness of the Church's Members

So much for "holiness of principles". It is time now to turn to "holiness of members". Does applying the criterion of a holy membership enable us to advance in establishing the claim that the "holy Church" of the Creed is to be sought in the Church body whose centre of unity is the bishop of Rome? Once again, relevant arguments can be marshalled by way of that trio of concepts internal to the idea of holiness: "common holiness", "more perfect holiness", "heroic sanctity".

Under the rubric of "common holiness" one might discuss whether the tendency of the Catholic Church to transform the general ethical temper of a culture in an evangelical direction is more apparent than with other Christian bodies, when the range of churches and ecclesial communities is scanned by the cultural historian. It is for Church historians to venture a judgment. Such is the complexity of the historical process (or processes) involved, that no great clarity of conclusion can perhaps be expected on this score. An English author will note, however, the losses sustained by the fabric of life of communities and of the poor in the destruction of guilds and monasteries in the sixteenth-century

Reformation. And if two wider generalisations may be ventured, I would suggest that in Protestant cultures there has been a narrowing of the range of virtues recognised as desirable (the word *bourgeois* might come to mind here), while in Orthodox cultures the corresponding diminution has been a much weakened sense of international solidarity typical of a universal Church.

More progress might be forthcoming from applying the category of "more perfect holiness". Arguably, the life of the evangelical counsels, and the spirit of that life when found among laity and diocesan clergy, has favoured a special degree of devotedness and disinterestedness, and thus an expansion of supernatural living, among the personnel of the Catholic Church. (I add that in this context it becomes pellucidly clear, should any doubt survive, how much harm scandals caused by religious and a celibate clergy do to the claims of the Church at large.) The capacity of the Catholic Church to put forth new religious orders to meet fresh needs in the pursuit of charity—a capacity certainly not disabled today, even in the difficulties that have attended the Church situation in the wake of the Second Vatican Council—exemplifies that "inexhaustible fecundity in all good" the First Vatican Council linked so closely to the mark of holiness.

Then there is "heroic sanctity": the Church as the Mother of manifest saints. Michel makes much of the way the heroic virtue of the saints is exposed to general inspection by the procedures of the Roman Church, which sift evidence that in principle anyone, believer or unbeliever, can verify. Canonisation procedures certainly carry more epistemological weight in evaluating the mark of holiness than does the erstwhile recognition of saints by popular acclamation. The claim can also be made that where the aggregate of features proper to Catholic Christianity is diminished by schism or heresy, the phenomenon of heroic sanctity diminishes likewise. If that claim be justified, it would follow that the docility of Christians towards the understanding of salvation found in the Catholic Church and their willingness to use the means made available there for growth in personal holiness, is a proper condition for the existence of a multitude—a stream, not a trickle—of heroically holy persons.

Such apologetic arguments for the identity of the (Roman) Catholic Church with the Church of the Creed logically entail that one will be able to discern the non-identity with the *Una Sancta* of the dissident churches and ecclesial communities. Classical apologetics seeks to show, in fact, that certain principles integral to the constitution of these non-Catholic traditions *specifically in their separateness* have a tendency to discourage the full flowering of sanctity.

Thus, for instance, Protestantism's perennial temptations to an anti-dogmatic rationalism on the one hand, and an illuministic individualism on the other, are, if followed out, major obstacles to the development of holiness. That was an argument commonly deployed in favour of some version of Catholic Christianity, whether Anglican or Roman, during the Oxford Movement.

Again, it might be argued that the doctrine of justification by faith alone, *fide sola*, which has some claim to be the founding principle of the sixteenth-century Reformation, is of its nature inimical to the growth of holiness in the Church's members. On a Lutheran-type understanding of justification, the practice of works of supererogation with a view to attaining perfect charity could be regarded as not only useless but even harmful to Christian existence— which is why securing the maximum precision in Catholic-Lutheran Agreed Statements on this issue is so especially desirable. The suppression of monasticism by the Reformers may be cited as an obviously pertinent example of a faulty soteriology at work.

With the Eastern churches separated from Rome, the position is rather different. Here the principles of sanctification are the same, though questions may be put about a certain weakening of their application through slight differences in doctrine and sacramental practice—for instance, in the lack of frequent Eucharistic reception (though, to be sure, frequent reception has its own snares) and a semi-secularisation of sacramental marriage (thanks to the permissions given for divorce and remarriage).

These considerations aside, it is at any rate arguable that the schisms between the Catholic Church and the various Eastern churches not united with Rome have not notably intensified the phenomenon of sanctity in those churches (so the schisms cannot find, by appeal to the mark of holiness, any theological validation). At the same time, the absence of procedures of canonisation fully comparable to what is found in the Church of Rome in the second and third millennia somewhat undermines the publicly evidential value of the saints of the separated Eastern churches.

A Dogmatic Approach

What I have been saying so far in this chapter, through dependence on Neo-Scholastic inspiration, may sound dogmatic enough, at least in the common sense of that word. And yet I have in fact confined myself to that epistemological approach to the mark of holiness typical of theological apologetics.

Only now do I go on to treat the matter as an issue in

dogmatics proper, where our concern is more with the ontology of theological realities, with the nature of their being, than with how we come to identify that being, to know about it. Introducing that ontology in blunt terms, then is this question: How can the Church be said to be intrinsically holy when not only her ordinary faithful, going about their ordinary business, sin daily, but so also do those deputed by ordination or religious profession to act in her name, and that not least in the course of their ministerial or spiritual duties? This is a topic of special salience today when the media seem able to ferret out scandals enough to satisfy a Borgia pope.

The dogmatic issue at the heart of thought about the Church's holiness concerns the question of how a Church partly sinful in her members can also be described as indefectibly holy in her essence.

When we were looking at the mark of unity, we found that the Church cannot be described, theologically, as more foundationally many than one, or even as equally one and many (the Creed confesses *una Ecclesia* not *multae Ecclesiae* or even, for that matter, *una multiplex Ecclesia*). There is a parallel with the mark of holiness in this respect. If we are taking our marching orders from the Creed, it will not do to say, rather in the manner of the novelist Graham Greene, that the Church is primarily a company of sinners, nor to say with Lutheranism that she is equally *peccatrix et justa*, "sinful and righteous". These strategies simply abandon the control the Creed, the Symbol of faith, should always possess over any attempted theological elucidation of that Creed. The Church is primarily and foundationally "holy Church", so the sinfulness of many of her members—including her ministerial members—must find its explanation within this global affirmation.

Our discussion of the Church's unity led us, following cues in Augustine and Thomas, to think of the Church as *una mystica persona*, a single mystical personality. And with the help of Heribert Mühlen, we identified the Trinitarian ground of that personality's unity in the way the Holy Spirit functions as a single Person in many P/persons, *eine Person in vielen Personen*, namely, in Christ and those who belong to Christ since through faith and the sacraments of faith they are initiated into Christ's life. The question this raises now, in relation to the mark of holiness, runs like this: In the way the Holy Spirit unifies the Church vis-à-vis Jesus Christ, does he constitute her a corporate personality to which the attribute of holiness can at all times unconditionally be applied, even when individual persons, aggregated by the Spirit to her fellowship with Christ, continue to be active bearers of the sin of the world?

Even after baptismal regeneration and subsequently, therefore, to our justification by faith and Baptism, the effects of sin remain in us (so everyday experience teaches) in the form of concupiscence—the tendency of fallen humanity towards morally ill-chosen means and ends. In the redeemed, this tendency is not, though, invincible. It persists indeed as a stimulus to spiritual warfare. *To that extent*, it can be hailed, paradoxically enough, as material conducive to our glorification. Yet this warfare, which is not always victoriously conducted, is itself a struggle, sometimes unsuccessful, with the remnants of evil in ourselves and in the wider world. Certainly, the Church is not without sinners. But is she therefore not a "holy Church"?

Following Mühlen, we have already said, in discussing the *unity* of the Church, that the ground of that unity, in terms of the gracious God himself, is the Holy Spirit (one Person in many P/persons). What may be the implications

of this assertion for the *holiness* of the Church? In the case
of a human individual, sanctification involves a fresh presence of God's uncreated graciousness, leaving its effect—so
the Latin theological tradition maintains—in the form of a
created grace dynamically affecting the powers of that individual's soul. In that way grace supernaturalises our individual personalities. Moving from the domain of the redeemed
person to that of the community of redemption, may we
not, then, think here of the uncreated Person of the Spirit
leaving, by his graciously unifying activity, the created effect of a new supernatural corporate personality on earth?
Can we say that the Church has a personality that is, accordingly, always holy even when her individual members,
weakening or failing in the spiritual warfare of the Christian
life, are not?

In other words, to use the convenient vocabulary of the
Thomist lay theologian Jacques Maritain, may we not distinguish the Church's own "personality", *sa personne*, from
her "membership", *son personnel*? Must we not do precisely
this, since only if the Church is in some way a supernatu-
ralised corporate personality is Tradition licensed in speaking of her as "she"?[15]

The difficulty in grasping what is involved in the Church's
personality is rooted in what at the same time makes it im-
perative for us to describe her in this way. In her own personality, she exists only by the act of Christ purifying and
sanctifying her human members through the Holy Spirit. As
the Fribourg dogmatician Jean-Hervé Nicolas observed, the
act of Christ that continually constitutes the Church is precisely the act whereby those who compose the Church are

---

[15] J. Maritain, *On the Church of Christ: The Person of the Church and her Personnel* (Notre Dame, Ind.: University of Notre Dame Press, 1973); see also
Maritain, *The Peasant of the Garonne: An Old Layman Questions Himself about
the Present Time* (London: Geoffrey Chapman, 1968), pp. 175–89.

freed from their sins and cease to be sinners.[16] Accordingly
—and this is the key point—the sins the Church's members
commit after aggregation to her unity are not committed by
them *qua members of the Church*: not (that is) qua persons who
are one person with Christ in the Holy Spirit. Such sins are,
rather, committed by us qua those *who are not yet unitively aggregated to her in fullness*. If we *were* so aggregated, we should
be entirely purified and sanctified: in a word, *holy*, and there
would be in us neither spot nor stain nor source for scandal.

In an idiom borrowed from Aristotle (and used for a purpose he could never have imagined), one might say that the
sins we commit we perpetrate not as the human "matter"
from which the Church is made, but as the "matter" from
which the Church draws out her faithful by *trans*forming
them: by conferring on them a new Christ-given, Spirit-
mediated, form of life. This is true also of her ministerial
members even (*pace* those clerical scandals) in their ministerial actions. A priest soliciting in the confessional, a pope ex-
communicating someone against the demands of the virtue
of justice: such Christians are, on these occasions, not acting
qua members of the Church but qua those who are yet to
become fully aligned with her.

What should we make, then, of the celebrated (or noto-
rious) patristic image of the Church as a "chaste harlot",
casta meretrix? It is a phrase Origen of Alexandria coined
and Saint Hilary of Poitiers turned into Latin.[17] Is this ancient (ante-Nicene) image of the chaste prostitute simply
contradicted by the later affirmation *Credo in . . . sanctam
. . . Ecclesiam* of the Creed of Nicaea-Constantinople? No, it

---

[16] J. H. Nicolas, O.P., *Synthèse dogmatique: De la Trinité à la Trinité* (Fribourg:
Editions universitaires de Fribourg, 1985), p. 698.

[17] See for references and a fascinating discussion, H. U. von Balthasar,
"*Casta Meretrix*", in his *Explorations in Theology*, vol. 2: *Spouse of the Word*
(San Francisco: Ignatius Press, 1991), pp. 193–228.

is not "simply contradicted", because the holiness that qualifies the Church as a personality is always *repentant* holiness, and it is this truth that the chaste harlot image brings out. When we commit sins, we never do so precisely as members of the Church. But when we repent of our sins, when we become penitent, we do so as members of the Church such that the Church herself *can be said to be penitent in us.* Indeed, the Church can be said to be penitent for all her sinful members, even for those who are not at the present time actually penitent, and it is this aspect of herself that we find embodied in, for instance, those religious orders in the Church where vicarious penance and reparation for the sins of others characterise a shared spirituality. Notions —and practices—of doing penance for the sins of others and offering up the fruits of one's own repentance for the conversion of sinners (historically speaking, well-developed themes in Catholic spirituality) make sense because through these behaviours one aligns oneself with the personality of the Church as the penitently holy Bride of Christ (chaste harlot) and so participates in the action of Christ in saving sinners. That act, as realised in us through the Holy Spirit, is, we have claimed, the dynamic foundation of the Church's *personnalité.*

In the first chapter, it was noted that the marks of the Church can be thought of not only epistemologically and ontologically but also (pedagogically and) eschatologically. The eschatological dimension stands in need of highlighting in the case of the mark of holiness.

To say that the Church is essentially holy—to assert that she is constituted by the act of Christ, mediated through the Holy Spirit, in freeing her members from sin, is not to say that her holiness is as yet of a consummate and definitive kind. The Church's initial holiness, in the opening moments of her existence—usually identified as Calvary when the Church was born and the Cenacle when at Pentecost she was manifested—this initial holiness of the Church is, to be sure, already recovered innocence. It is already complete freedom from sin. But this same initial holiness is also the starting point of an open-ended movement of coming to share more fully in the holiness of Christ, which itself will come to term eschatologically in the final Kingdom. After all, a newly baptised infant is certainly holy: regenerate, newly innocent. He is in a condition that parallels the Church's initial holiness at her own beginnings. But such a child is not yet a great saint.

This distinction between the ontological and the eschatological interpretations of the mark of holiness led the French Oratorian theologian Louis Bouyer, longest lived representative of the *nouvelle théologie* of the 1950s, to counsel speaking of holy Church now as the Betrothed of Christ (cf. 2 Cor 11:2) rather than his Bride, which she will be only eschatologically, in a future state; she has a waiting period of purifying preparation before she arrives at the celebration of the Wedding Banquet of the Lamb (cf. Rev 21–22).[18] For Bouyer, the pilgrim Church is, after the fashion of Israel in the oracles of the Old Testament prophets, a fiancée who has not yet arrived at the altar—in the Church's case, this will be the altar of the heavenly sanctuary. Bouyer is making a valid point, but he leaves behind the crucial text from Ephesians that is the charter of marital imagery in ecclesiology: "[A] man shall leave his father and mother and be joined to his wife, and the two shall become one flesh. This is a great mystery, and I mean in reference to Christ and the Church"

---

[18] L. Bouyer, *L'Eglise de Dieu: Corps du Christ et Temple de l'Esprit* (Paris: Cerf, 1970), p. 607.

(Eph 5:31–32). In any case, even a bride who is never un-faithful—as the Church qua Church is never unfaithful—can still be said to grow in perfect love for her husband. So we can affirm a relative unfinishedness to the bridal compact without relegating the Bride of Christ to the status of mere fiancée.

Bouyer's proposal to revise the traditional language along these lines can itself be reformulated in the light of Saint Thomas' commentary on the best-known wedding in the Gospels: the marriage feast at Cana. That wedding banquet signifies *mystice*, "mystically" (so Thomas writes), the union of Christ and the Church. The marriage is a reality and is rendered public when the Church unites herself to Christ by faith (which she does, one might add, at the moment of the Paschal Mystery, from Calvary to Cenacle). But, Thomas urges, this marriage will not be actually consummated—brought to its full completion—until the Bride is "intro-duced into the Bridegroom's nuptial chamber, in the heav-enly glory".[19]

One question remains, though, to be answered. In the Church's condition as Bride of Christ, how was her ante-riority to her own members—the priority of *la personne* in relation to *le personnel*—actually achieved? The Church, af-ter all, could never have existed and acted *except through par-ticular people*. When we speak of the Church as a personality that is not the same as her personnel, we do not mean that this personality can be found in total abstraction from her concrete membership.

Here we might think, following Nicolas, of the *aposto-lic community* being immediately sanctified by the Spirit of Christ in the Upper Room at Pentecost, so that the unfail-

---

[19] Thomas Aquinas, *Lectura super Joannem* 2:1.

ing mediatorial action of the Church—holy Church—in initiating people into holiness begins with the apostles and on their foundation.[20] This would link the mark of holiness to the mark of apostolicity, which I shall be considering in the next chapter.

Alternatively, however, we might prefer, with Hans Urs von Balthasar, to think of the Church as brought into existence *precisely as holy Church* in the Blessed Virgin Mary: not as convened with the apostles in the Cenacle, but in her own person and exclusively and by the Cross. In her role at the Cross, Mary was the locus where Israel, *Synagoga*, already the elect daughter of Zion (and the betrothed of God), became *Ecclesia*, the Bride of Christ. On this second view, holy Church as a personality existing in distinction from her personnel was immediately embodied not so much in the apostles but in her first and most eminent member, the Mother of the Lord. That is why in a book coauthored with Joseph Ratzinger, later Pope Benedict XVI, Balthasar called Mary the "primal" or "primary" Church.[21]

That option does not link the mark of holiness very obviously to any other mark of the marks given in the Creed. But it does have the advantage of finding a satisfactory context for the transition noted by Bouyer between the People of God as the Lord's Betrothed and the same people as his Bride. The rebetrothal of Israel to the Lord, a rebetrothal this time unbreakable, happened not on Calvary but in the mysteries of Mary's preparation for her Childbearing: the Immaculate Conception and the Annunciation. But the fiancée actually *became* the Bride on Calvary, when through Mary's faith, hope, and love, now reconfigured by

---

[20] Nicolas, *Synthèse dogmatique*, p. 698.

[21] H. U. von Balthasar and J. Ratzinger, *Mary: The Church at the Source* (San Francisco: Ignatius Press, 2005).

the Sacrifice of the Cross, holy Church as the Mother of sinners—but not herself sinful—came to be. That would also be a good basis, incidentally, for a theology of the Mother of God as Co-Redemptrix of the human race.

3

THE CATHOLICITY OF THE CHURCH

Introduction

Unlike the unity and the holiness of the Church, her mark of catholicity is not actually stated in Scripture in so many words. In Christian literature, the earliest appearances of the word *catholic*, as a qualification of "Church", comes from second-century sub-apostolic texts: the Letters of Saint Ignatius of Antioch[1] and *The Martyrdom of Polycarp*.[2] The word *katholikos* derives from the secular Greek phrase *kath' holou*, meaning (literally) "according to the whole", or, as one might say, "holistic". Scholarly opinion is divided as to whether the primary emphasis in Ignatius and the anonymous writer who wrote the Polycarp martyrdom text lies on the qualitative aspect of the notion of holism—in which case, likely English renderings of *katholikos* might be, for example, "authentic", "integral", "pure"—or, alternatively, on the quantitative aspect—in which case, the natural English translation for *katholikos* would be "universal".[3]

---

[1] Ignatius of Antioch, *Smyrnaeans*, 8.2.
[2] *The Martyrdom of Polycarp*, subscription; 16.2; 19.2, where the meaning "integral" seems more likely.
[3] Ibid., 8.1, where the meaning "universal" seems more likely.

Qualitative or Quantitative?

More generally, that distinction between qualitative and quantitative senses of the word is useful to keep in mind when tracing the development of a doctrine of catholicity in the ancient Church. Painting with very broad brushstrokes, the Greek Fathers seem to have held a mainly qualitative idea of what *catholic* means, the Latin Fathers, mainly a quantitative one. But that is only a rough-and-ready rule of thumb. Saint Augustine, for example, a Latin writer for whom catholicity is in the main quantitative, the word means communion with the Church as spread throughout the world. In it qualitative sense, the word stands for the holistic or total way in which the Church spread throughout the world entertains the Christian faith.[4] Again, Saint Cyril of Jerusalem, in the celebrated *Mystagogical Catecheses* preached in the church of the Anastasis, details five reasons why the Church is called "catholic". Of these, four fall under the heading of qualitative catholicity. Cyril says that the Church is catholic because she teaches all the doctrine needed for salvation; because she brings into her obedience every kind of man; because she has available the cure for every sort of sin; and because in her members she possesses every kind of virtue. And yet the reason for calling the Church catholic that he places at the top of his list is undoubtedly an example of quantitative catholicity. The Church, declares Cyril, is called catholic because she extends to the ends of the earth.[5]

In the subsequent history of theology, emphasis has laid now on the qualitative, now on the quantitative aspect. Thus

---

[4] Augustine, Letter 93, 23.
[5] Cyril, *The Mystagogical Catecheses*, 18, 23.

for instance in the Western Catholicism of the Counter-Reformation and the Neo-Scholastic tradition, *catholicity* means the wide geographical extent of a single sacramental society, which is plainly one thanks to the unity of its governance. Here the mark of catholicity is closely linked to the mark of unity within a basically quantitative concept of its application.

By contrast, for the nineteenth-century German Tübingen School (and this was a major influence in such makers of the Second Vatican Council as Yves Congar), catholicity is primarily qualitative and has to do with the way the divine life is integrally mediated through the sacramental economy of the Church. Again, in more recent Catholic writers influenced by the Eastern Christian tradition (including modern Orthodoxy), the Church's catholicity may well be explained chiefly in terms of the apostolic faith as handed down from the Fathers. And this, once more, exemplifies the qualitative emphasis.

Catholicity at Its Source

In the best contemporary theologies of the Church's catholicity, the attempt is made to relate this mark of the Church to the Church's own triune source in Jesus Christ. That is a plausible undertaking since parallels already exist in the way the Church's divines have explained the marks of unity and holiness. As we have seen, the mark of unity should be linked to the uniqueness of the divine plan as envisaged by the Father who, with the Son and the Spirit, the agents of the divine economy, is the one God of the Creed. And as we also saw, the mark of holiness is connected with the holiness of God as communicated by the Father's Spirit on the basis of the redemptive action of Christ.

When we come to the mark of catholicity, the connexion —between catholicity and God himself—is by no means so obvious. Relating the mark of unity to the unity of God and his plan is fairly obvious. Relating the mark of holiness to the holiness of the Spirit of Father and Son is entirely obvious. (The New Testament calls the third divine Person the "Spirit of holiness" [Rom 1:4].) What is not so obvious is how to ground the catholicity of the Church, through Christ, in the divine Trinity, for we do not usually speak of the "catholicity of God".

The American Jesuit Cardinal Avery Dulles, in a comprehensive account of this mark of the Church, sought to accomplish the not-so-obvious.[6] The divine pole of catholicity, Dulles proposed, is what Christian Scholasticism called God's "plenitude of being". That is a concept already found in the New Testament, where in the Letter to the Colossians (2:9) Paul speaks of the "fulness of deity", *plêrôma tês theotêtos*. That is an expression which historians of religion have sometimes regarded as a borrowing from Gnostic or proto-Gnostic vocabulary. But in fact, the idea of the divine fullness is already clearly articulated in the Hebrew Bible, as when, for instance, the voice of God enquires in an oracle in the book of the prophet Jeremiah, "Do I not fill heaven and earth?" (23:24).

Closely relevant to this fullness, for Dulles, is the way that, in the light of the New Testament revelation of God as Trinity, the divine unity can be said to be rich with the maximum differentiation possible to the divine nature. Father, Son, and Spirit, the three Hypostases that later theology, pondering the New Testament texts, will define in terms of

---

[6] A. Dulles, *The Catholicity of the Church* (Oxford: Clarendon, 1985).

their "mutually opposed" relations,[7] are themselves inner differentiations of the divine life, which, far from impairing the unity of that life, bring about in God the greatest possible intimacy of self-possession. God's plenitude as, specifically, the triune God, is the identity between, on the one hand, God's unity and, on the other, the relational communicativeness of his being in the maximal richness of life that is the communion of Father, Son, and Spirit. That identity is the true foundation of God's plenitude, and, according to Dulles, it justifies our speaking of the "divine catholicity", "the catholicity of God".[8] But from this point, we have somehow to get to the catholicity that concerns us more immediately in this book: the catholicity of the Church.

Trinitarian theology can only be related to ecclesiology via Christology and pneumatology. The reason for saying so is that the Church does not derive directly from the absolute Trinity but from the economic missions of Son and Spirit in the Incarnation and at Pentecost.

Catholicity and the Mission of the Son

Let us take first the mission of the Son. In New Testament context, the point of that Colossians text about the "fulness of divinity" was Saint Paul's claim that in Jesus Christ the *plêrôma* of the deity exists bodily. And this is patently a reference to the Incarnation. Because it communicates plenitude, dispensing as it does the fullness of divine grace and

---

[7] Thus, "paternity" and "filiation" (mutually opposed relations) conjoin Father and Son; "passive spiration" and "active spiration" (mutually opposed relations) conjoin the Spirit with the Father and the Son.

[8] Dulles, *Catholicity of the Church*, p. 32.

truth (cf. Jn 1:77), the Incarnation can be called the primordially catholic event in the history of creation. As the seventeenth-century poet Richard Crashaw, one of the English Metaphysicals, put it in his *Hymne of the Nativity*:

> Welcome, all Wonders in one sight!
> Aeternity shutt in a span.
> Summer in Winter. Day in Night.
> Heaven in Earth, and God in Man.[9]

In the Incarnation, the way the divine unity coincides with the maximal differentiation of the Persons in their distinction is echoed in a new way in the unity of Christ, who not only in his divine nature expresses the interrelation with himself of Father and Spirit, but also in his divine Person holds within himself the divine and the human natures that are his. And with that human nature of his there is necessarily bound up all the levels of created being that contribute to that nature—chemical, vegetable, sentient, rational. The Word incarnate has, then, a catholicity all his own.

Still remaining with the mission of the Son, there is something yet more to say. Our grasp of the catholicity of Jesus Christ should be amplified when we consider how he is not just in his divine nature the source of creation and in his human nature a complex example of it. He is also the Head of all creation: the One in whom, as preexistent, the world was made and by whom, as now humanised, the world is to be saved, that is, brought to a new pitch of operation, the Christ descends in his Incarnation and ascends as the glorified risen Lord with the end that he might "fill all things" (Eph 4:10). This process is not yet complete, but it is anticipated in the sacramental economy of the Church. Only at

[9] *The Complete Poetry of Richard Crashaw*, ed. G. W. Williams (Garden City, N.Y.: New York University Press, 1970), p. 83.

the Parousia (to which the Church's Liturgy looks forward with expectation and longing), when Christ hands over the finished creation to the Father (cf. 1 Cor 15:28), will the universe be totally penetrated by the catholicity of God.[10]

So far, however, in our Christological excursion, we have scarcely mentioned the Church, which is our real subject. Now we must note that, while the Pauline corpus teaches the headship of Christ over all creation, it also maintains that in far more intimate fashion Jesus is Head of his Body the Church. Despite what contemporary, ecologically minded, theological cosmologists might wish to assert, the New Testament never describes the universe as even potentially, through Jesus Christ, the "body of God". Cardinal Dulles gives those who would say so a firm smack: "There is no statement in Paul that the cosmic and angelic powers, though they be subject to Christ, belong to his body."[11] It is the Church, not the cosmos, that is Christ's Body, terminology intended to insinuate that Christ not only transcends the Church as her Head but is also interior to her: dwelling interiorly in the Church's members as they in him, and in that fashion constituting with them (as we saw in Chapter 1) "one mystical person". Now, when Christ, the Church's Head, communicates himself to her, the Church shares accordingly in the divine fullness and so comes to possess that fullness by participation. The Church is, then, "catholic" through participating in the catholicity of God in Jesus Christ. This she is already, even if imperfectly, since she can also be said, and by the same apostle, to be growing gradually towards the "measure of the stature of the fulness of Christ" (Eph 4:13).

---

[10] Dulles, *Catholicity of the Church*, p. 36.
[11] Ibid., p. 39.

The richly diversified unity of the Church—her catholicity—is especially apparent for Saint Paul in the variety of ministries and other vocations within her. Typically, Paul speaks of the risen Christ distributing a variety of ministries and callings for the building up of his Body so that its members can grow in the knowledge of the love of God that surpasses all knowledge and thus be filled, as the apostle puts it, "with all the fulness of God" (Eph 3:19). In First Corinthians, he discusses such ministries and callings in the widest possible context, which is that of the *charismata*. Charisms are divine gifts made not for individual edification (unless certain sorts of mystical charism be an exception here) but for the construction of the Body of Christ. Ordained ministry in the Church requires such charisms, and it receives them, but they are far from being confined to Holy Orders. The consequent endless multiplicity of vocations in the Church needs unifying, and this Paul ascribes in the Corinthian correspondence to the action of the Holy Spirit.

Catholicity and the Mission of the Spirit

Here I turn to the way that pneumatology, thinking about the Holy Spirit, also forms (with Christology) a necessary point of connection between Trinitarian theology and ecclesiology where the mark of catholicity is concerned. Though Balthasar (whom we encountered in connexion with the Church's holiness) is right to say that the Church has "the measure of its catholicity, which permeates and informs it, . . . in the mystery of Christ",[12] theological tradition has not been content with regarding the catholicity of the Church

---

[12] H. U. von Balthasar, *In the Fullness of Faith: On the Centrality of the Distinctively Catholic* (San Francisco: Ignatius Press, 1988), p. 16.

in *exclusively* Christological terms—in what Congar would call "Christomonistic" terms—that leave the Holy Spirit, intentionally or not, out of the picture.[13]

In the Church, persons are drawn into a communion that leaves intact both their differences as individual subjects and the particularity of the vocations that help define them. The communion concerned is unbreakably one—as well as on the inter-personal, and thus inter-vocational, level maximally diverse. This wondrous state of affairs (no other social body can rival it) strongly suggests that the immediate divine agent operative in the Church's catholicity is the Holy Spirit. The reason for saying so is that the Spirit has the same kind of role in the divine Trinity—to unite the Persons in communion without bringing about the slightest confusion between them.

Catholicity of ("Baptised") Cultures

In the case of the catholicity of the Church, the rich diversity held within unity is not just that of persons or individual vocations. It is also that of cultures and, indeed, of local churches within the unity of the single universal Church. By "cultures" I mean patterns of human living, styles of thinking, and kinds of sensibility when all of these are found together as corporate wholes.

The marvel the Spirit accomplishes in the Church is to foster communion without effacing differences, not just on the level of individual persons but also on that of baptised cultures as well. That is true within the Western Catholic

[13] As Balthasar himself recognizes when he goes on to write: "A Church can be Catholic only because God is Catholic first, and because in Jesus Christ *and ultimately in the Holy Spirit*, this catholicity on God's part has opened itself to the world", ibid., p. 29; italics added.

church (the Latin church in France, for example, has different strengths and weaknesses from the same church in Germany), but it is especially clear in the distinction between the Latin church and the Eastern Catholic churches, where diversity of rite, spirituality, and theology adds to differences of custom and outlook at home and in the diaspora. What results, by the Spirit's action, is not anarchy, or mere patchwork, but coherent diversity. That diversity is typified by inner contrasts but not by outright contradictions. Naturally, I exclude here as theologically unworthy of attention all pathological situations where Church life becomes, until suitably adjusted, heterodox and heteropractic. In ceasing to be Catholic with an uppercase *C*, such situations exclude themselves from the purview of catholicity with a lowercase *c* in the *una Ecclesia*.

Catholicity of Churches

What, then, of catholicity as touching the multiplicity of local churches? Thanks to the manner of the Church's internal structuring, the universal Church subsists as a nexus of local churches. The relation between the one Church and the many churches became as delicate an issue in the decades following the Second Vatican Council as had in the decades preceding it the issue of the "one mystical person" and the many individual persons who compose that corporate personality. That is why the concept of the Church as a communion suddenly shot into prominence as the way of steering the Bark of Peter through shoals, even though, so far as vocabulary is concerned, the idiom involved is largely absent from the documents of the Council itself. The Council does not have a prominent ecclesiology of communion. What people claim as evidence for such—key passages where the universal Church is said to be fully present in each of the local churches of the *Catholica* (*Lumen gentium*, no. 26; *Christus Dominus*, no. 11)—might be better described as offering an ecclesiology of epiphany: the universal Church epiphanises, or, in less dramatic terms, makes herself present, in each of those local churches of the Catholic world.

Reasons for emphasising the significance of the local church certainly exist. First of all, that significance follows from the embodiedness of men, who, despite the Internet, are still partly defined by their inhabiting of physical space. Territoriality is important for us. As people, we need a local habitation and a name. If the ecclesial economy is to transfigure the human, it must do justice to that. On the other hand, as we can see from such examples as ritual churches coexisting on the same territory (in Cairo there are, I believe, six or seven Catholic bishops of different such churches: Latin, Melkite, Coptic, and so forth),[14] and from personal prelatures like that of Opus Dei or the Military Ordinariates,[15] the concept of territoriality is not all-decisive where the local church is concerned. It is more correct to say that the local church is an ecclesial family or flock that normally but not necessarily takes territoriality as its instrument.

A second reason for emphasising the importance of the local church follows from Eucharistic doctrine. The manifestation of the Church Body is intrinsically related to the sacrament of the Lord's Eucharistic Body, and that sacrament

---

[14] The more correct expression is now "churches *sui juris*" (literally "of one's own law"), but that is hardly self-explanatory nor does it trip off the tongue.

[15] Though a prelature, the Personal Ordinariate of Our Lady of Walsingham established by Pope Benedict XVI in 2011 would not be so clear-cut an example: it is confined to the territory of the island of Britain.

can only be celebrated in a given place. It is so celebrated in its own symbolic fullness when the bishop presides and preaches at a Mass where all the orders of the church—presbyterate, diaconate, laity—are represented, for then the *vinculum symbolicum* of the apostles' teaching, the *vinculum liturgicum* of the Breaking of Bread and the prayers, and the *vinculum sociale* of the charitable organism of the Church under the guidance of her pastors (the *vinculum hierarchicum*) are all in evidence.

True, there has been from time to time an attempt to develop a theology of the Eucharistic Congress (an occasional global mega-event), where bishops, priests, deacons, and lay faithful drawn from many parts of the world come together under the presidency of a pope or a legate appointed by him and dent somewhat the conviction that in principle the Eucharist can only be a celebration by a single local church. The exceptional nature of such congresses, though, might be thought to prove the rule.

Then thirdly, there is (in favour of accentuating the local churches) an argument from pneumatology of broadly the kind I have been developing under the rubric of the note of catholicity. The transcendence of the Spirit, who makes Christ and Christians one mystical person is best witnessed, it can be said, through the fullness of the legitimate diversity he inspires via the distribution of his many gifts, so that in the many churches, each with (in theory at least) its own distinctive life, the richness of his grace may be seen. It follows from the cumulative force of these arguments that producing a high theological doctrine of the local church is justified.

The question remains, however, whether in an account of the communion of the Church it can be justified to grant a position of priority to a theology of the local churches. This was the point at issue in the well-reported exchange between two curial cardinals, Walter Kasper and Joseph Ratzinger, shortly before the latter's election to the papal office.[16] It follows from what was said in the initial chapter of this study about the first mark of the Church, her unity, that the attempt to render Catholic theology primarily a theology of local churches in their interrelation must necessarily fail. The universal Church in her unity is not a product of the being of the local churches. Rather, she is an ontologically prior reality, founded on the impact made by the missions of Son and Spirit on the first disciples with, at their centre and in a crucial position (so we saw from the second chapter of this book), the Mother of the Lord. It is the Church thus founded that replicates herself with an infinite variety of nuance in a multitude of places and times.

Here are, moreover, three supporting arguments for the priority of the universal Church: one from the nature of Holy Baptism, one from the theology of the Eucharistic oblation, and one from the canonically acknowledged existence within the Church of what we may term "global institutions".

First, while at Baptism a candidate is received into a particular church community, he becomes more fundamentally a member of the Church universal. As Avery Dulles points out, this may be inferred because "Baptism can be validly administered where no community is present" and "some baptised Christians while lacking any stable relationship to a particular parish or diocese [for example, a group of Gypsies] are entitled to receive the sacraments wherever they go."[17]

Secondly, while it is true (with the seeming exception

---

[16] K. McDonnell, "The Ratzinger/Kasper Debate: The Universal Church and Local Churches", *Theological Studies* 63 (2002): 227–50.

[17] A. Dulles, S.J., "The Church as Communion", in *New Perspectives on Historical Theology: Essays in Memory of John Meyendorff*, ed. B. Nassif (Grand Rapids, Mich. and Cambridge: Eerdmans, 1996), p. 134.

already noted) that the Eucharist can only be celebrated in a particular or local church (i.e., a diocese or a parish or its equivalent), the Mass itself is essentially ordered towards the salvific good of the entire Church in whose name it is always offered. And thirdly, such institutions as ecumenical councils, the Petrine office, the episcopate considered as a college, and worldwide religious orders of the globally unified variety, can only with the greatest of difficulty be fitted onto the procrustean bed of a communion ecclesiology of a particularist kind, in which local churches are prior in significance to the Church universal.

It is sometimes said that the institutions of the universal Church are simply an emergency mechanism to be called on when the local church—in principle, self-sufficient—somehow goes wrong. But the principle of subsidiarity, which Catholic social thought applies to natural society, cannot apply in only that form to ecclesial society, owing precisely to the ontological anteriority of the universal to the local church. The responsibilities of universal leadership in the Church—by the college of bishops with the pope at their head or by the pope acting in his own name as successor of Peter—are inescapable if the Church is to possess a social unity of a kind that is capable of being the outward and visible sign of her spiritual unity as one mystical person.

Quantitative Catholicity

We might seem to have retreated from considering the mark of catholicity to looking again at the mark of unity. But what we have really done is to make the transition from the qualitative to the quantitative sense of catholicity. The self-diffusive fullness of God expressed through Christ and the Spirit in the Church is not only intensive, to do with a quality of human life under grace. It is also extensive, to do with the extension of that life to as many people—and peoples—as may be possible. This dimension of missionary outreach is where quantitative catholicity comes into its own.

Already in the Old Testament, the conversion of all the nations to the God of Israel was seen as the goal of the divine plan by the more universalist Hebrew prophets. The realisation of this promise would be the institution by Christ, under the impulse of his Spirit, of a single ecclesial society, characterised by universal outreach under divinely provided shepherds. During the public ministry, Jesus had looked forward to a future proclamation of the Gospel to the Gentiles, predicting that many would come from East and West and would sit down with Abraham, the prototype of the people of the promise (cf. Mt 8:10–12). Subsequently, the apostolic community regarded the sending of the Spirit of the risen Christ as the cue for the universalisation of Israel: for making Israel universal in the New Israel, the Church. When the evangelist Luke describes Peter's Pentecost sermon as heard in their own language by "devout men from every nation under heaven" (Acts 2:5), he evidently regards this as the apostles' receiving their marching orders for spreading the Gospel throughout the Mediterranean world and beyond— as is indeed described in the Book of Acts.

Again, in his Revelation, Saint John depicts an angel flying across the sky "with an eternal gospel to proclaim to those who dwell on earth, to every nation and tribe and tongue and people" (14:6). Above all, where New Testament references are concerned, we have the missionary command at the end of the Gospel according to Saint Matthew, what Evangelicals call, very appropriately, the Great Commission:

"Go, therefore, and make disciples of all nations" (28:19a), words that are echoed at the end of the Gospel according to Saint Luke (24:47) and in the so-called longer ending of the Gospel according to Saint Mark (16:16).

Now if the Church is the bearer of the Gospel and corporately its missionary embodiment, if she is (therefore) the sacrament of God's universally redemptive will in Christ, she must manifest an impulse to be extensively or quantitatively catholic and not just intensively or qualitatively so. If there is *one* Church, the *una Ecclesia* of the Creed, that Church cannot be identified with any body that defines its ecclesial mission in a quantitatively restricted way, by reference to particular races or nations. Nor can that one Church be identical with a body that is content to let other church bodies have exclusive occupation of particular regions of the planet's surface without reference to itself. If the Church were content to exist in some restricted portion of mankind, she would lack what Dulles calls "semeiological universality": universality in her capacity to be a sign.[18] *Vera Ecclesia* is duty bound to "trespass" (as critics would have it) on the territory of church bodies that define themselves in purely national terms.

All this presumes there is still somewhere on earth a Church that has inherited the apostolic mandate and responsibility. That is the question raised by the last mark of the Creed: *Credo in . . . apostolicam Ecclesiam.*

---

[18] Dulles, *Catholicity of the Church*, p. 74, citing the same author's *Dimensions of the Church* (Westminster, Md., 1967), p. 51.

4

THE APOSTOLICITY OF THE CHURCH

Introduction

When in the last chapter we looked at the catholicity of the Church, we found it took all the subtlety of intelligence of Avery Dulles to tie in the note of catholicity with some appropriate feature of the character of the Church's Source, the triune God in Jesus Christ. But for the fourth mark, the theme of the present chapter, nothing could be easier than to connect apostolicity with the missions of the Son and Spirit. The word "apostle" is from the Greek word meaning "a person sent forth". The sendings of Son and Spirit from the Father are, then, the archetype of the apostolic mission. It is through the way the Spirit and the Son are sent, and continue to be sent in the post-Incarnation, post-Pentecost economy of salvation, that the mark of apostolicity has (like the marks of unity, holiness, and catholicity) its Trinitarian matrix.

And as between that matrix, on the one hand, and the life of the Church today, on the other, there is a crucial link. It is of course *reference to the holy apostles themselves*. When we speak of the Church's apostolicity, we have in mind the Church's fidelity to everything given the apostles as a sacred trust to equip them for that mission. So the question we must set ourselves to answer here is this: To what might that "everything" refer?

Defining Apostolicity

In *L'Eglise une, sainte, catholique, et apostolique*, Yves Congar opens his section on apostolicity with a crisp definition. Apostolicity "is the property thanks to which the Church preserves across time the identity of her principles of unity as these were received from Christ in the persons of the apostles".[1] What he has in mind turns out to be the content of the three principles we looked at in discussing the mark of unity, namely, the three bonds of communion: the *vinculum symbolicum* of unity in doctrine; the *vinculum liturgicum* of unity in sacramental life; the *vinculum sociale aut hierarchicum* of unity in social life under the guidance of pastors who have inherited their ministry from the apostles. Apostolicity is concerned with the preserving intact of these principles over the period of time that has elapsed since the apostles themselves.

Apostolicity has to do then, in the first instance, with relation with the Dominical past, that is, the past stemming from the Person and work of Jesus Christ and notably his founding the Church on the apostles. As Congar puts it, the Church exists by a kind of expansion of the original apostolic group,[2] which is why writers of the second century are so keen on showing, over against Gnosticism (chiefly), the continuity of the churches with their apostolic founders. The drawing up of lists of bishops also attests to this, for, as we shall see, the succession of apostolic ministers plays an important part in the continuing apostolicity of the Church.

It should not be thought, however, that apostolicity is exclusively concerned with such a relation to the past—even

---

[1] Y. Congar, *L'Eglise une, sainte, catholique et apostolique*, (Paris: Cerf, 1970), pp. 181–82.

[2] Ibid., pp. 187–88.

the Dominical past. The Twelve, the inner circle of the New Testament apostolate, have in the Gospels, and in the Revelation of Saint John, a further, eschatological significance. In the Lucan recension of the words of Jesus, they will sit on twelve thrones of judgment, just as in Revelation their names are inscribed on the foundation stones of the heavenly Jerusalem. The Covenant made by Jesus Christ, who is Alpha and Omega, and communicated via the apostles, is a new and everlasting Covenant which entails the gift of a share in final salvation: the *ultimate* good God has in store for man. The beginning of the apostolic fellowship looks forward, then, to its fulfillment—in history and beyond—at the Eschaton. In this sense, the purpose of apostolicity is to unite the Church's beginning to her last end. It is to assure the continuity of the saving revelation from the first, hidden, coming of Christ to his second and glorious coming. Thus apostolicity has a reference to the eschatological future as well as to the Dominical past. I have criticised Bishop John Zizioulas for a certain conflation of Christ and the Church—but I must give him full marks here for the admirable way in which he underlines this future reference.[3]

Apostolicity Viewed as a Distinguishing Mark of the Church

When the mark of apostolicity is approached apologetically, however, in its epistemological character, as a way of identifying among the multitude of human societies claiming the Christian name, the *una sancta et catholica Ecclesia* of the Creed,

---

[3] For his theology of apostolicity, see J. Zizioulas, "Apostolic Continuity and Succession", in his *Being as Communion: Studies in Personhood and the Church* (New York: St. Vladimir's Seminary Press, 1985), pp. 171–208.

emphasis is necessarily placed on relation with the past. The reason for that is simple. Relation with the Eschaton, the absolute future, is hardly verifiable just now.

Whereas mediaeval theologians had comparatively little to say about apostolicity (they were in any case generally assuming, as the framework of systematic thinking, the Old Roman Creed, which, paradoxically, despite its traditional name—the Apostles' Creed—has no mention of the apostolicity of the Church), later on, Catholic polemicists of the Counter-Reformation and beyond made a great deal of this particular mark, apologetically speaking. Usually they held the mark of apostolicity to have three aspects: first, the Church's apostolicity of origin; secondly, her apostolicity of doctrine; and thirdly, the apostolicity of the ministerial succession of her hierarchs. We shall be looking at the second and third of these shortly, but meanwhile I offer a brief historical sketch of how concern with the first, apostolicity of origin, came to develop.

Development of Concern with Apostolicity of Origin

"Your Church goes back to Luther or Calvin, ours to the apostles" was the basic argument from apostolicity in the post-Reformation period, although the question "Where was your Church before the Reformers?" was sometimes combated by Protestants with the counterquestion, "Where was your face this morning before you washed it?" Such apologetic concern with apostolicity of origin was not, though, altogether new. It had some primitive precedents. It is found in the age before Nicaea—with Cyprian, in Tertullian and Irenaeus, and even in Clement of Rome, who perhaps was writing before the close of the New Testament period itself (before the last book of the canon of Scripture was completed).

It is, therefore, unsurprising that people soon wanted to fill in the lexical gap in the Old Roman Creed and, indeed, in the earliest form of the Creed of Nicaea. They wanted something about apostolicity put in. In 451, the fathers of Chalcedon ascribe to their predecessors at Constantinople I, the second ecumenical Council, which had met seventy years earlier, an expansion of the Nicene Creed that includes the key word *apostolic*. On the Church's behalf, so the bishops at Chalcedon reported, the conciliar fathers had expressed their faith in the *apostolikê Ekklêsia*. And they had done well in so doing.

If the mediaeval *Summa* tradition had little or nothing to say on this topic (I have mentioned that typical authors were not, in general, following the literary outline of the Nicene-Constantinopolitan Creed), we should not draw the false inference that, unlike the fathers of Constantinople I, the mediaevals considered the Church's apostolicity of origin to be unimportant. Instead, the importance of the topic in their eyes comes over in other ways. In Saint Thomas, for example, the idea is expressed by the notion of the Church's *firmitas*: her permanence or solidity, which he ascribes to her foundation on the apostles, teaching as she does the same doctrine as the apostles themselves.[4] Here the apostolicity of the Church's origin is treated as, in effect, the same thing as the apostolicity of her doctrine. The concealed premise, evidently, is the assertion that only a body originating from the apostles could both know their teaching and indefectibly persevere in it.

On occasion, however, mediaeval writers were obliged to

[4] Thomas Aquinas, *In Symbolum apostolorum expositio*, art. 9.

confront the issue more directly, owing to the rise of anti-ecclesial sects such as the Cathars and Waldensians, for these claimed to have revived the apostolic inspiration and way of life. In dealings with such groups, Catholic spokesmen such as Eckhart of Schoenau or the Dominican Moneta of Cremona could hardly avoid the topic.

Nevertheless, it was in the age of the Counter-Reformation that expositions of the Church's apostolicity came into their own. Surprisingly, perhaps, the Reformers themselves seem to have addressed the theme of apostolic origin comparatively rarely. It is never mentioned in, for example, the 1541 edition of John Calvin's *Institutes of the Christian Religion*. Rather, it was their Catholic critics who discovered it as a powerful controversial tool, that is, against those Reformed theologians who still maintained that the Church is a visible communion and not just an invisible community of the predestined. A non-Catholic divine who had retained from the corpus of patristic and mediaeval theology the notion that the Church and her ministry are media of saving grace linked to the incarnate Word via the apostles was obviously accessible to this argument. The Church—that is, *vera Ecclesia*, the true Church—must be apostolically originated.

At the very least, any body of Christians who could be shown not to possess the doctrine of the apostles could by that token be shown not to be apostolic in origin and hence not constituting the apostolic Church of the Great Creed (an example of that negative mark thinking described in my opening chapter). First formulated by Catholics, it was an argument, so Protestants—and especially Anglicans—found, that could be turned back against spokesmen for the old religion. While Catholics might not have subtracted from the faith of the early Church, they had surely added to it—

which was almost equally bad. Rome, so it was said, had abused apostolic Christianity by illegitimate accretions to its doctrinal substance. Famously, this was the line taken by the Tractarians, including the early John Henry Newman, during the Oxford Movement. Newman's theory of the development of Christian doctrine was his attempt to answer that case—in other words, to defend the apostolicity of the Church of Rome.

As I have already mentioned, under the heading of the Church's apostolicity, theology gathered together three themes: apostolicity of origin, apostolicity of doctrine, and apostolicity of ministers. Though in principle these themes are distinct in practice, the first tends to be discussed in terms of either the second or the third or both of these together. Thus I shall consider myself justified in moving swiftly on to the remaining duo.

Apostolicity of Doctrine and Ministers

While the idea of the apostolic succession is the idea of the continuing presence of the apostolic origin of the Church, that continued presence, and therefore that succession, may be looked at in terms of either doctrine or ministers, or— as is best—in terms of both at the same time.

The notion of the apostolic succession as a succession of ministers—of, above all, bishops, with the pope at their centre, and, by derivation from the papal-centred episcopate, of presbyters and deacons, is likely to be uppermost in the minds of Catholics who have had a classical catechetical formation and know something of the historical or indeed contemporary background in disagreements, or attempted ecumenical agreements, with Anglicans, Lutherans, and others. "You haven't got the apostolic succession!" is the cry of polemical triumph against such separated Christians (who in the case of many Anglicans and some Lutherans, notably in Sweden and Finland, may want to argue, "Oh yes, we have!").

In one sense, the succession of ministers is a fuller expression of apostolicity than is apostolicity of doctrine. The continuity of the apostolic succession of ministers, expressed in the ordination of bishops who are incorporated thereby in the apostolic college "under and with Peter" (and this Petrine aspect is missing even among the separated Eastern churches), has as its purpose—its intrinsic finality—not just the preservation of Christian doctrine in its integrity but also the assurance in the Church of a true sacramental worship. Christians are initiated into the apostolic succession of ministers so as to ensure the purity and integrity of the faith of the People of God, specifically as that faith is professed in Baptism and in the other sacraments. Hence, the purpose of extending the apostolic succession by the episcopate (and to a lesser degree, the presbyterate) is to secure *the entire confessional and liturgical structure of the Church as a whole.*

The manner of Jesus' final commissioning of the Twelve after the Resurrection shows that we are dealing with a ministry that is simultaneously one of evangelisation and sacramental reconciliation with God: "Go therefore and make disciples" (evangelisation); "baptising them" and "forgive the sins" (sacramental reconciliation). This is more than simply assuring the continuance of the apostolic faith.

At this juncture, however, we need to introduce a qualification. True, the succession of ministers in the Church is rendered apostolic by the continuous transmission of the episcopate from the apostles through the laying on of hands.

And yet the topic of the ministerial succession from the apostles cannot be disjoined from the issue of the conservation of the doctrine transmitted by the apostles. Unfortunately, ministerial succession can be perpetuated as a bare fact without conserving the right faith in right worship—in a word, the *orthodoxy*—which is its *raison d'être*. Thus, for instance, the fact of the preservation of the apostolic succession by the Old Catholics of the Union of Utrecht or among the Syrian Jacobites does not necessarily render one or more of these bodies identical with the *apostolica Ecclesia* of the Creed, for the question has to be addressed: Do the bishops of these bodies teach what the apostles, explicitly or implicitly, taught?

In this perspective, apostolicity of doctrine becomes the litmus test for adjudicating claims to that specific apostolicity of ministers that renders a church substantially identical with the apostolic Church confessed in the Creed. Even the pope, let alone the bishops, is not apostolic in the sufficient sense required unless he is teaching the apostolic faith. That is why theologians have discussed, prudently and sometimes imprudently, by what means an individual pope might by words as well as actions defect from his apostolic office— for instance, by personally denying the already defined faith of the Church. The ministerial succession is, it may be suggested, first and foremost, though not simply and solely, succession on a chair of teaching—in Latin, *cathedra* or *sedes*, in Greek *proedria*.

Until Constantine, the special seat of a bishop was the only outward sign of his episcopal dignity. To succeed to the apostles is, as the mediaeval authors who touched on this subject were well aware, to succeed above all to doctors or preachers of the faith. There is a certain circularity here. As the historian of doctrine Jaroslav Pelikan remarks, drawing into the circle the not unrelated question of the apostolicity of scriptural texts:

> The definition of the apostolic norm as apostolic scriptures interpreted in accordance with apostolic tradition by those who stood in apostolic succession was, of course, an argument in a circle; for one could determine what were apostolic scriptures by comparing their contents with apostolic tradition and by consulting the usage of the apostolic sees, which one could identify by checking their scriptures and by verifying their doctrines—and so all the way round. Yet it did imply a working view of how the various theories of normative self-definition could become instead the components of a single, though composite, theory.[5]

The essential link between apostolic doctrine and apostolic ministry explains why no one can take on a ministerial function in the Church without making a profession of faith. No bishop, at any rate, can be ordained without making such a profession, nor can a duly ordained bishop enjoy voting rights at an ecumenical council without renewing it. These practices are pointers to the underlying theological reality involved. The teaching of the bishops acts as a rule for the faith of Catholic Christians, yes. But the teaching of the bishops is itself rule-grounded. It is conditioned by their fidelity to the apostolic tradition as conserved and actualised in the Church under the guidance of the Holy Spirit. That is why the faithful have a duty to reject bishops—even when lawfully elected (appointed) and ordained —who alienate themselves from the authentic succession

[5] J. Pelikan, "The Two Sees of Peter: Reflections on the Pace of Normative Self-Definition East and West" in *The Shaping of Christianity in the Second and Third Centuries*, vol. 1 of *Jewish and Christian Self-Definition*, ed. E. P. Sanders (London: SCM Press, 1980), pp. 57–73, here at p. 73.

by erroneous teaching, namely, that which fails to meet the criteria of congruence with what is taught in other local churches of the Catholic Church and notably in the church of the city of Rome in which, as Irenaeus puts it, "there has always been conserved that which is the tradition from the apostles".[6]

And we can cite there not just the Roman church and other apostolically founded churches such as Antioch but also local churches with no apostle as their direct founder since, as Tertullian explains, local churches that have no apostle as their founder are no less apostolic than those who do if they preserve with the latter "consanguinity of doctrine".[7] Post-apostolically founded churches like the church of New York or the church of Birmingham profess the same faith as their apostolically founded sister churches—the church of Rome or of Antioch—because they have the same stream of the apostolic teaching coursing through them.

A helpful maxim runs, "The content of the succession is the tradition." When we talk about the apostolic succession of ministers (bishops), we should not have in mind what Lutherans rightly stigmatise as a *nuda successio*, a "bare succession", otherwise unexamined, of one bishop to another, according to formally correct sacramental and canonical procedures. Rather, we should be talking about a succession that transmits the content of Tradition unimpaired and in its fullness.

That useful axiom contains another clause which shows us the other side of the coin. If Tradition is the content of the succession, then the succession is the form of Tradition.

---

[6] Irenaeus, *Adversus haereses*, III. 3, 2. The best study of this important text is probably E. Lanne, "L'Eglise de Rome, *a gloriosissimis duobus apostolis Petro et Paulo fundatae et constitutae Ecclesiae*", *Irénikon* 49 (1976): 275–322.

[7] Tertullian, *De praescriptione*, 32.

Tradition is not found outside the community defined by the ministerial apostolic succession. And that means we cannot go all the way with the Lutherans in their more-or-less exclusive emphasis on apostolicity of doctrine and associated disapproval of Catholic reliance on the tactile succession: the succession of ministers from the apostles through the laying on of hands. It is sometimes said that reliance on a tactile succession, a thread of contact coming down through history by the laying on of first apostolic and then episcopal hands, is a kind of materialism. If so, it is a distinctively Christian sacramental materialism that fits well with the nature of the Incarnation itself.

The hiatus between the Paschal Mystery and the Parousia implies a will on the part of the Word incarnate that his apostles should, as and when necessary, incorporate others into their mission. He willed that they should entrust to these others the *traditio* of his teaching as brought to mind by the Holy Spirit, as well as the Gospel signs—above all, Baptism and Eucharist—which are the sacraments of the Kingdom. He willed that this should happen by a gesture of commissioning until his return in glory. This is what the claim that Christ instituted the apostolic ministry in fact means. This is how Saint Paul, in the Pastoral Letters to Timothy and Titus, understood things.

We may not be able to establish what the content of the apostolic tradition—and notably apostolic doctrine—is except by identifying that Church which *by the way she possesses the apostolic succession of ministers can show herself to be apostolic in origin* and thus the Church of the Creed. The form that is the ministerial succession can guide us to the apostolic tradition's content—even though it is also true that to lack the content means to be left only with a form. Once again, we are within a circular argument. But not all circles are vicious circles; some are virtuous.

Corollaries of Apostolicity

Some corollaries of the theology of apostolicity need underlining. First, though the bishops succeed to the ministry as equals of the apostles qua pastors of the local churches with the responsibility to build up the confessional and liturgical structure of those churches, bishops, unlike apostles, enjoy no charism of divine revelation. They are powerless to constitute a new normative tradition, a tradition (in other words) that is not just an explication of the revelation of which the apostles are the final mediators and definitive witnesses.

The "charism of truth" (to take a phrase from Irenaeus) received by the bishops is not a capacity to initiate new authoritative teaching.[8] It is, rather, a gift of teaching what the apostles explicitly or implicitly taught—a gift which, in the case of the Roman bishop alone, brings with it a personal charism of infallibility in defining such teaching—which is, by that very fact (be it noted) not a capacity to *add to* the revelation given by the apostles.

Secondly, the only *clear* case of an apostolic minister succeeding in a personal way to the pastoral office of an apostle concerns Peter and Paul, on the one hand, and the Roman bishops on the other. Otherwise, bishops are said to succeed to the apostles corporately, by enrolment in the *coetus* or *collegium*—the "group" or the "college"—of the apostles: terms borrowed by the Second Vatican Council, with some

[8] Irenaeus, *Adversus haereses* IV. 26, 2.

earlier precedent, from Roman civil law. A pointer to that is the practice, mandated by the first ecumenical Council, of ordaining bishops at the hands of multiple consecrators —classically, three.

A grey area in Catholic ecclesiology is in what sense bishops in apostolically founded sees like Antioch can be regarded as in some kind of personal episcopal succession by (partial) analogy with what is held *de fide* about the See of Rome (the analogy cannot be complete for lack of a claim that Antioch was confirmed in faith by the *blood-witness* of Peter).

Thirdly, the convocation of bishops around the pope continues sacramentally the gathering of the original apostolic college around Peter. But, as I said, it also anticipates the City that endures forever, founded as it is on the apostles of the Lamb. From the terms in which Jesus addresses the Twelve, the key figures of the apostolic group, it is plain that he intended them to have a share in his Lordship over the Church as inaugurated by the initial coming of the Kingdom at Easter but not consummated until the final judgment. The Liturgy sees the Twelve as continuously present to the Church of the in-between times through the ministry of the bishops who are now their vicars. The apostolic ministry makes the pope and bishops living icons of the Twelve around Peter in their irreplaceable role of shepherding the flock of God. As the Preface of the Apostles in the Roman rite puts it, addressing itself unusually to the Son, not the Father: "It is right and just humbly to beseech you, Lord, not to abandon your flock, O eternal Shepherd, but by your holy apostles to keep it continuously under your protection that it may be governed by those shepherds you established at its head as vicars of your work." The document, prepared jointly by a body of Catholic and Orthodox theologians in the United States, notes appositely that the eschatological dimension of apostolicity

> does not only mean that the Church, founded on the Twelve, awaits its perfect form at the end of God's plan for history. It also means that the Church shares now in the finality, the irrevocable fullness, of God's action within the changes of history, precisely because the Twelve have passed on to the Church their witness to the presence of God's kingdom in the risen Lord and their role as authoritative heralds of his coming in history.[9]

Calling the pope—even a bad pope—Peter *redividus*, showing a bishop religious honour by kissing his ring (something managerially minded administrator bishops find an embarrassing irrelevance): these customs of speech or gesture are not mere popular piety. They are an appropriate response in rhetoric and action to the sacramental figuring that pope and bishop perform in the Church on the apostles' behalf. As two French theologians, writing jointly, have put it: "This apostolic succession is not a dynastic succession to disappeared apostles. It is, rather, the permanence of the apostles' presence in the same ministry received from Christ."[10] It is because the apostles preserve their transcendence vis-à-vis the bishops—the bishops do not replace the apostles, they "stand in" for them—that, to cite the Frenchmen again, "the theme of the succession is only the historic trace [the signal, or give-away sign] of the eschatological status of the apostles in the Church."[11]

---

[9] *Apostolicity as God's Gift in the Life of the Church*, no. 6, cited in H. M. Biedermann, O.S.A., "Apostilizität als Gottes Gabe im Leben der Kirche", *Ostkirchliche Studien* 37 (1988): 38–54, here at p. 39.

[10] J. M. Garrigues and M. J. Le Guillou, "Statut eschatologique et caractère ontologique de la succession apostolique", *Revue thomiste* 75 (1975): 395–417, here at p. 399.

[11] Ibid., p. 403.

If this is correct, then the association of the bishops with the apostles is more intimate than their historic succession one to another. In the so-called Liturgy of Hippolytus—a guidebook for the worshipping acts of the Church passed down, significantly, under the title *The Apostolic Tradition*—the ordination prayer for a bishop speaks of him as united to the apostles in the same loving plan that the Father conceived in Jesus Christ. Elsewhere that deliberately conservative third-century author writes in the name of the episcopate at large: "We are the successors of the apostles to whom it has been given to participate in their self-same grace of priesthood and teaching, to be the guardians of the Church."[12]

---

[12] Hippolytus, *Elenchos*, cited in ibid., p. 405.

PART II

HER MASTERS

5

HENRI DE LUBAC

Introduction: A Quartet of Theologians

My quartet of masters in the figuring out of the Church has not been selected at random. *Henri de Lubac*, an influential *peritus* at the Second Vatican Council, found in its Dogmatic Constitution on the Church, the charter for a recovery, in ecclesiology, of the mind-set of the Fathers.[1] The constitution rapidly established itself—hardly surprisingly—as the normal departure point for contemporary Catholic ecclesiology in the postconciliar epoch. *Jean-Marie Tillard*, the most junior of the four, can be described as taking further certain features of de Lubac's ecclesiology, with a particular concern for the reunion of the churches, notably in the context of Catholic-Orthodox relations. *Hans Urs von Balthasar* was deeply influenced by de Lubac, of whom he wrote a book-length study (they were cofounders of the journal *Communio*). Balthasar's thinking about the Church, concerned in this area, as in others, to recuperate what he deemed a threatened Catholic identity, might be considered a critique of ecclesiology practised in the setting of the ecumenical dialogues, a warning not to neglect the *distinctively* Catholic

[1] H. de Lubac, S.J., "Lumen Gentium and the Fathers of the Church", in *The Church: Paradox and Mystery* (Shannon, Ireland: Ecclesia Press, 1969), pp. 30–67.

themes. Lastly, *Charles Journet*, who, as a Neo-Scholastic, is by far the most systematic of these writers, stands appropriately for a classically *Latin* Catholic *organisation* of those themes—as well as others shared with Christians who look to the Great Church of history for their inspiration, notably the Orthodox and Anglo-Catholics. Thanks to Journet's systematic bent (though his ecclesiological *opus magnum* is incomplete and never found a satisfactory literary form), an account of his doctrine also serves as a suitable way to round off this study.

In each case, I shall be interested in the way this quartet of figures amplify, by considerations drawn from the wider resources of the deposit of faith, an account of the Church structured in terms of her four marks—unity, holiness, catholicity, apostolicity. What they have to say about those themes will confirm the importance accorded them in the present book.

De Lubac: His Life

Who, in short compass, was the first of my masters, Henri de Lubac?[2] Born in 1896, he was a Jesuit most of whose early formation took place in the Society's residences for French members in British exile. That was owing to the legislative restrictions the Third French Republic had imposed, for secularist reasons, on the religious orders. Returning definitively to France in 1926 (he had served for a period in the French Army during the Great War), de Lubac was soon accepted into the inner elite of the Catholic intel-

---

[2] For a fuller account of his life and work, see A. Nichols, O.P., "Henri de Lubac: Panorama and Proposal", *New Blackfriars*, 93, no. 1043 (2012): 3–33.

ligentsia. Professionally, he taught fundamental theology at the Institut Catholique in Lyons and went on there to be the first occupant of a chair of the history of religions (his publications would bear witness to both these aspects of his work).

In 1940, in collaboration with his confrere Jean Daniélou, he started the collection *Sources chrétiennes* for the (semi-) popular divulgation of patristic texts. After the German invasion that same year, he played a major part in the spiritual resistance against Nazism in Occupied and Vichy France. In the period immediately following the Second World War, he enjoyed considerable influence as both editor of the journal *Recherches de science religieuse* and adviser to a prestigious series of monographs in historical and dogmatic theology entitled, simply, *Théologie*.

As a result of the crisis over *nouvelle théologie*, a movement of thought marrying two enthusiasms, the Greek Fathers and modern philosophy, de Lubac was removed from teaching by the Jesuit authorities in 1950. But in 1960, his fortunes changed when Pope John XXIII, who as apostolic nuncio in Paris had known of de Lubac's travails, named him a consultor of the commission preparing the Second Vatican Council. Much employed as a *peritus* during that Council, he devoted a good deal of time lecturing internationally on the true sense of its teachings—warning, notably, against turning the Council into what he termed a "para-Council", an "absolute point of departure for drawing the Church in an unjustified direction", in rupture with her past.[3] He was

---

[3] G. Chantraine, "Lubac, Henri de", in *New Catholic Encyclopaedia: Jubilee Volume; The Wojtyła Years* (Washington: Gale Group: 2001), pp. 345–48, here at p. 346. That judgment about his intentions is amply confirmed by H. de Lubac, *L'Eglise dans la Crise actuelle* (Paris: Cerf, 1969), and *Entretien autour de Vatican II* (Paris: Cerf, 1985).

created a cardinal by Pope John Paul II in the consistory of 1983. Henri de Lubac died in 1991, leaving quite a raft of publications behind.

His Writings

Apart from the topics already mentioned, de Lubac's writings concern Greek patristics, mediaeval exegesis, Renaissance philosophy, the theology of grace, and, not least, ecclesiology. His contributions to the latter straddle the conciliar divide. To the years before the Council belong *Corpus mysticum* in 1944 (though he brought out a new edition in 1968)[4] and *Méditation sur l'Eglise* in 1955;[5] the period after the Council saw *Paradoxe et mystère de l'Eglise*, from 1967,[6] and *Les églises particulières dans l'Eglise universelle* in 1971.[7] Portions of others of his published works are also highly germane to his ecclesiological thought: notably *Catholicisme: Les aspects sociaux du dogme*, a deathless classic from 1938,[8] and, appearing in 1969, *La Foi chrétienne*, an exposition of the Apostles' Creed in the light of its deep form (and a work

[4] H. de Lubac, *Corpus mysticum: The Eucharist and the Church in the Middle Ages* (Notre Dame, Ind.: University of Notre Dame Press, 2007).

[5] H. de Lubac, *The Splendour of the Church* (London and New York: Sheed and Ward, 1956). This translates the second, 1953, edition of the French original.

[6] H. de Lubac, *The Church: Paradox and Mystery* (Shannon, Ireland: Ecclesia Press, 1969).

[7] H. de Lubac, *The Motherhood of the Church* (San Francisco: Ignatius Press, 1982). I have access only to the French original, *Les églises particulières dans l'Eglise universelle, suivi de 'La Maternité de l'Eglise'* (Paris: Aubier-Montaigne, 1971).

[8] H. de Lubac, *Catholicism: Christ and the Common Destiny of Man* (London: Burns, Oates, and Washbourne, 1950), translating the fourth, 1947, edition of the French original.

to which I shall need to refer at the end of my account).[9] Conveniently, he also brought out a substantial memoir explaining what he thought he was doing in writing his various books.[10]

His Approach to Ecclesiology

How does de Lubac approach ecclesiology? And, within that wider question, what does he have to say about the four dimensions of the Church signalled in the Creed? Though de Lubac was not a systematic writer, Balthasar at least considered his master to have produced an "organic life-work".[11] While de Lubac never brought his ecclesiological reflections into a single interrelated whole, brave souls may attempt that for themselves.[12] In the space available for my four portraits, only a modest version is possible.

Catholicity

In *Catholicisme*'s chapter "The Church", de Lubac opens by espousing a strongly qualitative view of catholicity. The Church, he insists, "was already catholic on the morning of Pentecost".[13] Hence—so de Lubac argues—catholicity

[9] H. de Lubac, *The Christian Faith: An Essay on the Structure of the Apostles' Creed* (San Francisco: Ignatius Press, 1986).

[10] H. de Lubac, *At the Service of the Church: Henri de Lubac Reflects on the Circumstances that Occasioned his Writings* (San Francisco: Ignatius Press, 1993). I use for this the French original: *Mémoire sur l'occasion de mes écrits* (Paris: Culture et Vérité, 1992).

[11] H. U. von Balthasar, *Henri de Lubac: Sein organisches Lebenswerk* (Einsiedeln: Johannes Verlag, 1976).

[12] See, for instance, H. Schnackers, *Kirche als Sakrament und Mutter: Zur Ekklesiologie von Henri de Lubac* (Frankfurt: Lang, 1979).

[13] De Lubac, *Catholicism*, p. 14.

cannot be primarily quantitative, to do with geographical extent or statistics. He understands qualitative catholicity in a way that stresses the roots of the word, which in Chapter 3 I termed "holism". The Church is catholic because, in relation to God, she makes mankind whole.

At the same time, de Lubac would link the mark of catholicity to the mark of unity. By gathering people to herself, the Church renders mankind whole again not least by restoring the organic unity in which man was originally created. When the Church is manifested at Pentecost, tongues of fire proclaim a gift of tongues for speech to come. But the point of that gift is not so much to predict the future extension of the Church to different nations. Rather, it is to declare the Tower of Babel finally undone, as mankind understands itself again to be a single family in God.

That "in God" is important. In his concern for remaking the unity of man, de Lubac is not an early harbinger of liberation theology or a spokesman for the providential character of the United Nations organisation. The progress he envisages is by way of a spiritual revolution, producing, via the Church, a deeply God-centred world. *Catholicisme* was a highly influential work in the Roman Catholic Church of the 1940s, '50s, '60s. Looking back, de Lubac suggested it was a pity that little attention seemed to have been paid to the last of three adjectives he used to define its approach, which was not only "social" and "historical" but also "interior".[14]

In *The Church: Paradox and Mystery*, he refined his account of the mark of catholicity so as to rub in that "interior" dimension. There can be in the Church no "wholeness", no qualitatively universal catholicity, without the recentering

---

[14] De Lubac, *Mémoire sur l'occasion de mes écrits*, pp. 25–26.

of man in God. The Church, he writes, is "catholic, that is, universal [because] she wishes her members to be open to everything and yet [he continues] she herself is never fully open except when she is withdrawn into the intimacy of her interior life [and] in the silence of adoration".[15] This strong, and even perhaps excessive, statement was surely fuelled by the fear that qualitative catholicity was increasingly understood in humanistic terms, terms inimical to the dimensions of contemplation, worship, and mysticism in the Church's life.

The Church as "She"

I note that Henri de Lubac habitually refers to the Church as "she". He approved of that early document of Roman Christianity *The Shepherd of Hermas*, whose author portrays the Church as a woman "created before all things".[16] With any ecclesiologist who refers to the Church as "she", it is always worthwhile to ask why. At the most basic level, so de Lubac would answer, the personification of the Church as a woman denotes the close bonding that typifies the Church's social being—as with calling Israel a woman in the Hebrew Bible. Indeed, for de Lubac, the Jewish nationalism that finds expression in various parts of the Old Testament and dogged the steps of Jesus when he sought to explain Messiahship was a necessary piece of anticipatory symbolism if the redeemed were to understand how salvation is essentially social: how it comes about through *her*, the Catholic Church.

Yet the story does not end there. The deeper reason for calling the Church "she" lies in the relation between the

---

[15] De Lubac, *Church: Paradox and Mystery*, p. 3.
[16] Hermas, *The Shepherd*, Vision 2, 4.

Church and the Blessed Virgin Mary. In Mary, so de Lubac writes in *The Splendour of the Church*, "the whole Church is outlined, and at the same time already completed; she [Mary] is simultaneously the 'seed' and the 'pleroma' of it."[17] The Mother of the Lord, in other words, is both the Church's matrix and the Church's fullness.

In a striking comparison with patristic Christology, he speaks of a veritable "communication of idioms" taking place between our Lady and the Church.[18] Just as the union of divinity and humanity in the single Person of Christ enables one to ascribe to him as God what, strictly speaking, belongs to his humanity, and to him as man what, strictly speaking, belongs to his divinity, so the unity between Mary and the Church is of such a kind that each can be described in terms that, strictly speaking, belong to the other. Here the social unity of the Church is thought of as preconstituted in the grace given to Mary. For de Lubac, no profounder rationale for referring to the Church as "she" can be conceived. Judging by the way they root the holiness of the Church in the Mother of God in *Mary: The Church at the Source* (cf. Chapter 2 above), Balthasar and Ratzinger could only agree.

The Church as Mystery and Society

To de Lubac's mind, Christ's redemptive act in the Paschal Mystery, on the one hand, and, on the other, his foundation of the Church community, make up together one single saving action. And this explains why the Church is at once a mystery and a society—invisible and visible at one and the same time. As he writes, "She [the Church] is a mys-

---

[17] De Lubac, *Splendour of the Church*, p. 259.
[18] Ibid., p. 249.

tery surpassing its outward manifestations."[19] Following the
cue of *Lumen gentium*, he always begins with the Church as
mystery. In *The Church: Paradox and Mystery*, he identifies
the mysterial dimension of the Church by saying that she is
a reality "coming from God and entirely at the service of
his plan. [She] is an organism of salvation, precisely because
she relates us wholly to Christ and apart from him has no
existence, value or efficacy."[20]

Only secondarily is the Church a society—able to be investigated as are other societies—in the service of salvation.
And yet just as the humanity of Christ is held together with
the divinity in his single Person and in the manifestation
of that Person in his saving work, so too in her duality of
aspects—the human society and the organism of salvation
—the Church is unconfusedly yet inseparably one. "The
Ecclesia de Trinitate [Church from the Trinity], whose hier-
archic mission has its origin in the divine processions themselves is also, under the other aspect, the *Ecclesia ex hominibus*
[Church from men], and this indissolubly so."[21]

De Lubac employs a rich variety of ways to express this
state of affairs and to draw out its implications. I confine
myself to three of them. The first is philological: to do with
how we are to understand the word *Church*. Commenting
on the derivation of the word *ekklêsia* from the Greek verb
for "call" or "convoke", de Lubac claims that the Church
is logically prior to those who are called. "She is a *convo-
catio* before she is a *congregatio*."[22] She is more primordially
the mediatrix of the Gospel than she is the fellowship of
those who have heard the Gospel. Here he can be found

---

[19] De Lubac, *Catholicism*, p. 22.
[20] De Lubac, *Church: Paradox and Mystery*, p. 15.
[21] De Lubac, *Splendour of the Church*, p. 71.
[22] De Lubac, *Catholicism*, p. 20.

arguing the toss with classical Protestantism, for which only the Word of God (and therefore not the Church) convokes whilst the subsequently "gathered" believers come together to make a (or the) church. For de Lubac, however, it is the Church who summons through the grace of the Word, and not only summons but also generates, or gives life to, new Christians.

This leads us to his second manner of commenting on the unique position of the Church as at once the continuance of the redemptive mystery and also (in dependence on that mysterial foundation) a visible society with its own characteristic human practices. From his earliest ecclesiological essays until his last, he was preoccupied with the thought that the Church is not only a woman, she is a Mother.[23] Bringing together numerous patristic texts on *Ecclesia mater*, he finds them summed up in a poet of the late-nineteenth-century Catholic revival, Paul Claudel. Claudel gave thanks for refinding faith in the words, "Blessed be that mother at whose feet I have learnt all."[24]

Towards the end of his life, in the lengthy essay "The Motherhood of the Church", de Lubac confessed that the analogy between the Church and a human mother limps, but only because the Church is more "maternal" than any mother, not less so. Not only does she "give us birth in the new life she carries by receiving us into her bosom". Over and above this, "the more our divine education progresses, the more intimately are we linked to her."[25] That is the opposite of what we generally find in parenting, where the more the child profits from the mother, the more he becomes independent of her. Unlike Nicolas, whose account

[23] Ibid., pp. 4–5; de Lubac, *Splendour of the Church*, pp. 174–207.
[24] Cited in ibid., p. 23.
[25] De Lubac, *Les églises particulières dans l'Eglise universelle*, p. 161.

of the holiness of the Church in terms of the act aggregating members to her by purifying them (see Chapter 2 above), de Lubac does not offer a dogmatic explanation of how a body that is our spotless Mother can have members (including ministerial members) with dirt and even blood on their hands. His response is, rather, a spiritual one: "Contemplating my Mother's humiliated face, I will only love her twice as much."[26]

But then thirdly, the relation between the redeeming act and the Church-society also warrants us calling the Church "the sacrament of Christ".

> If Christ is the sacrament of God, then the Church is for us the sacrament of Christ; she represents him, in the full and ancient meaning of the term, she really makes him present. She not only carries on his work but she is his very continuation, in a sense far more real than that in which it can be said that any human institution is its founder's continuation.[27]

That third way of expressing how the Church even as a visible society is an intrinsic aspect of Christ's redeeming work—the sacrament of Christ—led de Lubac to underwrite the most popular ecclesiological concept of his epoch, the Church as Christ's "Mystical Body", which we have already encountered when thinking about the mark of unity in Chapter 1 above. Whatever else it may be, the concept of the Mystical Body is clearly an example of extended sacramentality: the Church-Body is the graciously enabled sign of the activity of its divine-human Head.

De Lubac will agree with Congar and Ratzinger that to deemphasise Body-of-Christ ecclesiology for the benefit of

[26] De Lubac, *Church: Paradox and Mystery*, p. 9.
[27] De Lubac, *Catholicism*, p. 28.

People-of-God ecclesiology is a mistake.[28] While at the Second Vatican Council the dominance of Mystical-Body ecclesiology under Pius XII gave way to a new stress on the Church as the People of God, this carried with it the danger of reverting to an Old Testament account of the "assembly of God" in a quasi-Jewish ecclesiology insufficiently shaped by the Incarnation and the Paschal Mystery. As de Lubac put it, rather more diplomatically, in *The Church: Paradox and Mystery*: "Would it be excessive to see in the second chapter [of *Lumen gentium*, i.e., the chapter on the Church as the People of God] the fruit of a happy biblical movement, but one which has not yet fully explored in all its profundity the traditional dialectic between the two Testaments?"[29] That may be as close to criticising a conciliar text as a future cardinal is advised to go!

By and large, de Lubac writes about the Church as the Body of Christ in a way hardly distinguishable from the terms of Pius XII's great encyclical on this topic, *Mystici corporis Christi*. One can, however detect two distinctive de Lubacian nuances, of which the second will be more influential than the first. He places greater stress on how the Church only becomes fully the Body of Christ eschatologically, at the end of time.[30] And he opens up an aspect of Body-of-Christ thinking that is old in a way that is new. He sounds the overture of "Eucharistic ecclesiology" in the modern Catholic Church.

[28] De Lubac, *Church: Paradox and Mystery*, pp. 39–47.
[29] Ibid., p. 43.
[30] Ibid., pp. 26–27.

Eucharistic Ecclesiology

From his wide reading in the Latin Fathers and the mediaevals, de Lubac had noticed as early as the writing of *Catholicisme* that something slightly odd had happened to the language of Latin theology. Originally, it was the Church that was described as the "true Body" of Christ, the *corpus verum*, whereas the Eucharist was called the "Mystical Body", the *corpus mysticum*. Later (certainly by the time of Saint Thomas), these terms had switched reference. The Eucharist was now hailed as the true Body, the Church as its mystical counterpart. Unlike some commentators, de Lubac did not regard this development as sinister, an attempt to downplay the role of Eucharistic reception as unifying the body of worshippers—perhaps in favour of monastic elitism or clerical domination. On the contrary, de Lubac believed the doctrines involved to have remained stable under the—nonetheless striking—mutation of vocabulary.

What is at stake is, evidently, the relation between the Eucharistic sacrament and the Church as sacrament of Christ. In the words of one English student of de Lubac's thought,

> To describe the Eucharistic Body as the *true* Body of Christ, as we now do, tends to suggest scattering and vagueness as this "true" Body is distributed to feed the *mystical* Body. However, to describe the *ecclesial* Body as the *true* Body, as the Fathers did, immediately focuses attention on the unity of Christ and the Church, the unity served by the eucharistic Body (the body present in the liturgical mysteries, i.e., the *mystical* Body), and suggests the image of the latter [the Eucharist] as a centre of attraction concretely gathering the Church into one.[31]

---

[31] P. McPartlan, "Eucharist and Church, the Contribution of Henri de Lubac", *The Month* (1988): 847–59, here at p. 848.

Purely by chance, de Lubac had a perfect opportunity to follow through this intuition (at that stage, it could hardly be more). Going into work at the Institut Catholique, he found a note from the dean of the faculty saying he would be needed as second examiner for a thesis on the ninth-century theologian Florus of Lyons, about whom he knew nothing. Shortly after, convalescing from an illness at the Jesuit house in Aix-en-Provence where there happened to be a full set of the *Patrologia Latina*, he read through Florus' writings, and much more of the largely unstudied Carolingian theologians of Florus' time, discovering thereby the full extent of the connexion between Eucharist and Church made by these authors—a connexion that, afterwards, would be overshadowed by theologies of the Eucharistic Presence and, later still, the Eucharistic Sacrifice. Hence his own *Corpus mysticum*, the charter (we might well call it) for a Western Catholic Eucharistic ecclesiology.

Far from setting himself against the grain of contemporary magisterial teaching about the Church's nature, de Lubac thought his "discovery" would aid the understanding of Pope Pius XII's teaching in *Mystici corporis*. The pope had insisted that when we call the Church the "Mystical Body of Christ" we are not just speaking of a moral body, a body of people united by sharing the same intention, the "intention" of faith. (I touched on the deficiencies of such a thin approach when discussing the *vinculum liturgicum*, considered as a bond of unity, in my opening chapter.) Nor, Pius went on, by using the word *mystical* are we implying that the sense in which the Church is Christ's Body is somewhat obscure. For de Lubac, Pius XII might usefully have added that when the early mediaeval divines spoke of the Church as the "Mystical Body" they meant, helpfully, the body that is "mystically signified and realized by the Eucharist—in other words, the unity of the Christian community which is made real by the 'holy mysteries' in an effective symbol (in the strict sense of the word 'effective')."[32]

De Lubac's version of Eucharistic ecclesiology must be distinguished from other varieties of the species. His is not a systematically Eucharistic ecclesiology: he does not claim that the total shape of the Church can be read off from the Eucharistic celebration. Not everything that is true in ecclesiology can be inferred from the sacrament of the Eucharist. Though he liked and used the formula "The Eucharist makes the Church", he did not think the field of application of this maxim unbounded. As he wrote in *The Church: Paradox and Mystery*, the Church comes to a focus in the Holy Eucharist—but not only there.[33] The Church is also focussed in the saint—and indeed, one could add, given his preoccupations in later life, in the person of the pope.

Visible Structure

That leads by a natural progression to the question of how de Lubac understood the visible structure of the Church.

Whereas others might argue that the concept of the Church as a "Church of churches", a communion of episcopally presided Eucharistic assemblies, may be inferred from the *déroulement* of the Liturgy, de Lubac maintained that the visible structure of the Church must be sought by casting our glance more widely than simply looking at the Mass—vital though the latter is. By our reception of the Holy Eucharist,

[32] De Lubac, *Splendour of the Church*, p. 92.
[33] De Lubac, *Church: Paradox and Mystery*, p. 5.

we are not only joined more intimately to Christ, we are also incorporated more fully into the Church. And yet the being of the Church into which we are thus more profoundly absorbed is not to be discovered from the Eucharistic celebration alone. In *The Splendour of the Church*, de Lubac commented that while "Christ in his Eucharist is truly the heart of the Church", an organism does not consist of heart alone.[34]

More specifically, when de Lubac turned to deal with the apostolicity of the Church as found in a succession of ministers, he did not regard the episcopate, with the Roman bishop at its centre, as deriving from her Eucharistic life. He admitted that the principal task of the ministerial priesthood is the celebration of the Eucharist. And yet that priesthood enjoys a certain priority vis-à-vis the Eucharistic community. Without the apostolic office—without the episcopate and presbyterate—there could be no Eucharistic community. In his preferred terminology, the fatherhood of the Church's ministers is a privileged expression of the motherhood of the Church.[35]

From the standpoint of gender distinction, that sounds highly confusing—until we remember that (as already discussed) the Church's motherhood is one of de Lubac's ways of asserting the priority of the Church as continuation of Christ's redemptive act over against the Church as human gathering. What de Lubac is saying amounts to this: since the apostolic ministry is, like the Holy Eucharist, of direct divine derivation, it cannot be regarded as a product of the Eucharist but, instead, must be viewed as a precondition of

---

[34] De Lubac, *Splendour of the Church*, p. 113.
[35] De Lubac, *Les églises particulières dans l'Eglise universelle*, p. 193.

its celebration. A de Lubacian way to put that, curious as that may sound, is to confess, "The hierarchy is our mother." The notion of precondition is a useful one for understanding de Lubac's attitude to the Petrine office. The pope, he writes, is "the sign and condition of Catholic unity".[36] He is the guardian of the communion of the many different local episcopally ordered churches ("particular churches", de Lubac calls them, anticipating the language of the 1983 Latin Code). That is not something Eucharistic ecclesiology can tell us. We know it—if know it we do—from other courses, by other means. For de Lubac, we know it from Tradition, from the Church's memory as expressed in her practice. For the "mutual inclusion" of the one Church of the Creed and the multiplicity of local churches to be effective, there must be a unique centre to which Tradition "gives the names of Peter and Rome".[37]

Conclusion

Though de Lubac wrote on the topic of ecclesiology over a period of more than half a century, there is no noticeable change in his views. What alters is the context and the mood. In his early writings, he is painfully aware that many Protestant Christians consider Catholics to be ecclesiolaters, worshippers of the Church, who confound the visible institution with the whole work of Christ and give her hierarchs an homage due only to the Redeemer. Over against such misunderstandings, he insists that we do not believe in the Church in the same sense in which we believe in God.

At the end of his life, by contrast, de Lubac had to confront

---

[36] De Lubac, *Splendour of the Church*, p. 124.
[37] De Lubac, *Mémoire sur l'occasion de mes écrits*, p. 136.

a minimalistic ecclesiology among Catholics themselves, a scholarship for which it was fashionable to present an anarchic view of Christian origins, and an attitude for which it was perfectly acceptable to proceed by treating the Church as something we can make up as we go along. In his last ecclesiological essay, the entirety of an eighteen-page introduction is devoted to this problem.[38] His solution to the problem of postconciliar ecclesiological minimalism can be found in his study of the Apostles' Creed. His advice is this: explain to people that, while we do not believe in the Church as we believe in the triune God, nevertheless, the Church is the corporate subject—the individual-transcending subject —of all Christian believing. When as Catholic Christians we believe, we do so from start to finish by participating in the faith of the Church.[39] That comes to us first by hearing, in the apostolic preaching,[40] but then by a process of interiorisation,[41] as the voice of our ecclesial Mother gives her accent more and more to our own.[42]

---

[38] De Lubac, *Les églises particulières dans l'Eglise universelle*, pp. 7–25.

[39] De Lubac, *Christian Faith*, pp. 185–94.

[40] Ibid., pp. 194–95.

[41] Ibid., pp. 195–98.

[42] Ibid., pp. 198–201. For the implications for the task of the theologian, see p. 225.

6

JEAN TILLARD

Tillard's Life

Jean-Marie-Roger Tillard was born in 1927 in the French overseas *département* of Saint Pierre et Miquelon, two small islands in the Gulf of Saint Lawrence. After (so unconfirmed rumour has it) training as an actor, he joined the Canadian Province of the Order of Preachers when he was twenty-one. The imaginative flights and occasionally rather *outré* humour of his speaking style give the rumour of his histrionic past a certain plausibility, but these traits were allied with great theological seriousness, thus making a heady brew.

Tillard studied in Ottawa and Rome and at Le Saulchoir, the celebrated study-house of the Dominicans of the Province of France,[1] gaining doctorates in both theology and philosophy, though the latter discipline is apparent in his work chiefly in the form of a Cartesian lucidity in the presentation of theological ideas. As a professional teacher,

---

[1] Brief clues to his debts to particular Dominican teachers can be found in C. Ruddy, *Tillard and the Future of Catholic Ecclesiology* (New York: Crossroads, 2006), p. 4. A fuller biographical sketch can be found in G. D. Milhiot, "Le Professeur", in *Communion et Réunion: Mélanges Jean-Marie-Roger Tillard*, ed. G. R. Evans and M. Gourgues (Leuven: Leuven University Press, 1995), pp. 21–30.

he held the post of professor of dogmatics in the Dominican college at Ottawa for nearly forty years. He used that
post as a base camp from which to sally out for global lecturing, including prolonged stays in England, where he was
lionised by a number of Anglicans, owing to his ecumenical
activities in the service of the Pontifical Council for Christian Unity. He was a theological mainstay of the bilateral
dialogues between the Catholics and Orthodox, as well as
between Anglicans and Catholics; acted as vice president of
the World Council of Churches' Faith and Order Commission, where he played a notable role in the making of the
influential Lima Document *Baptism, Eucharist and Ministry*;
belonged at various times to the Pontifical International
Theological Commission; and was a member of the board
of the Ecumenical Institute at Tantur, in the Holy Land.
He died very suddenly, of hitherto undiagnosed cancer, at
Ottawa on 13 November 2000.

Tillard's Work

In contrast with de Lubac's, Tillard's work was chiefly ecclesiological in scope (the only other area to which he devoted much time was the theology of religious life). From
his first book-length study, *L'Eucharistie, Pâques de l'Eglise*,
written when he was in his early thirties, to *Eglise d'églises:
L'ecclésiologie de communion*, published around his sixtieth
birthday, it is always the mystery of the Church he has in
view. That would remain the case with his last publication,
L'Eglise locale: L'ecclésiologie de communion et la catholicité, from
1997. That work was self-consciously a challenge to those
who considered that, not least in the wake of the distur-

bance which characterised much of Catholicism following the Second Vatican Council, the most useful thing the "local church" (understood here as *diocese*) could do was to heed gratefully the stabilising signals it received from the Roman "centre". Some caveats about the prioritising of the local church have already been entered in Chapters 1 and 4 of the present work—suggesting how the topic is indeed something of a hot potato.

Not that Tillard was new to such controversies. Possibly his most influential book had been *L'Evêque de Rome*, dating from 1982, a study of "the pope . . . more than a pope?", which was rapidly translated into other languages. It is reported the writing of this book—which in its aim of rendering the Petrine office more acceptable to non-Catholic Christians happened to coincide with a major policy goal of Pope John Paul II—produced an invitation to contribute to the making of the 1994 encyclical letter *Ut unum sint*. In that document, whose publication was timed to prepare for the bimillennium of Christianity (in the year 2000), the pope invited other churches and ecclesial communities to make proposals for how, ideally, they would wish to see a universal primacy function in the Church at large. Response to the encyclical was somewhat disappointing—the opportunity seems to have been grasped more by dissident Catholics than by members of other ecclesial bodies, though the Orthodox lay theologian Olivier Clément was a significant exception.[2] The limited response does not necessarily annul, however, the significance of Tillard's contribution, to which I shall return.

---

[2] O. Clément, *You Are Peter: An Orthodox Theologian's Reflection on the Exercise of Papal Primacy* (Hyde Park, N.Y.: New City Press, 2003).

Eucharistic Ecclesiology Again

Tillard's early theology of the Church set out as a self-confessedly Eucharistic ecclesiology. "The Eucharist: Easter of the Church" begins from what Tillard called the "traditional" axiom, *Eucharistia facit Ecclesiam*. (The force of de Lubac's conviction that his favoured phrase, "the Eucharist makes the Church", summed up the sacramental ecclesiology of many of the Fathers gave more people than Tillard the impression he was recalling an actual patristic formula.)

Like de Lubac, Tillard meant in the first place by this formula the simple claim that the sacramental Body of the Lord builds up his Church Body. But he also gave his own inflexion to this affirmation in a spin that introduced two emphases that were relatively new.

First, for Tillard, the Eucharist is the Church's Easter: her way to share in the Lord's Paschal Sacrifice and his Resurrection triumph. It is also, consequently, the Church's way of sharing in what made that glorious Passover possible, a movement from the world of sin to the world of God, which is itself the world of perfect charity.

And then in the second place, through being the way the Church shares in the mystery of Easter, the Eucharist launches her on her way to the Kingdom. Eucharistic ecclesiology, in Tillard's eyes, is necessarily eschatological. Putting together these two special emphases—the Paschal and the eschatological—furnishes the Tillardian form of de Lubac's maxim. In Tillard's own words: "The sacrament of the Table of the Lord accomplishes the Easter of the Church on her march toward the eschatological Kingdom."[3] This is, then, a strongly sacramental ecclesiology: sacramental grace

---

[3] J. M. R. Tillard, *L'Eucharistie, Pâques de l'Eglise* (Paris: Cerf, 1964), p. 7.

courses through the Church-organism, or what Tillard calls the "ecclesial communion of life which the Lord Jesus pours out for his brethren".[4]

A Theology of Communion

The appearance in that statement of the word *communion* is prophetic for Tillard's later work. Indeed, even in this early monograph, he could write, "In what is deepest in her essence, the Church is nothing other than the communion of life which men have with the Father and amongst themselves, in Jesus Christ, by the Holy Spirit."[5] Salvation, for Tillard, *is* communion with God, and it is achieved by the events of the Incarnation and the Atonement, in the Cross, Resurrection, and sending forth of the Pentecostal Spirit of the enfleshed and crucified Word. Communion with the Father is communion of life in Christ and his Spirit in the Church.

It is hardly too much to say that Tillard virtually identifies the Church—understood as divine communion, not as human society—with salvation itself, frequently hyphenating the two words *Church* and *salvation* in the formula *Eglise-Salut*. Church and salvation are, in a phrase he is fond of, "inadequately distinct". The force of this (slightly shocking) quasi-identification is mitigated, though, by his distinction between what he calls the first and second "moment" or "time" in the coming-to-be of the Church.

The period between Pentecost and the present is the "first time of salvation in the Church", when the mystery of ecclesial salvation, which is present already in its intensity in

[4] Ibid., p. 57.
[5] Ibid., p. 36.

the Jesus of Easter, flows even now from and in the Church. Not, however, till a "second time", arriving only with the Parousia of the Lord, will the Church have "actualised in her members the plenitude of the Easter Jesus".[6] Thanks to this distinction of times, Tillard draws back from making the claim that the Church is the fullness of salvation now.

What happens in Tillard's later ecclesiology of communion is not that these themes make their retreat—the Paschal Mystery and especially Pentecost retain all their salience for him, and the Eucharist remains central. But he goes on to discover the significance of the theme of communion not simply for the salvation-relationship with God that the Church makes possible but also for exploring the Church's visible or organisational structure—not least in a perspective of ecumenism.

Under the pressure of ecumenical negotiations, Tillard felt obliged to give increasing attention not so much to the liturgical and mystical aspects of Eucharistic ecclesiology, which were the focus of his earlier work, but to its possible implications for the visible structure of the Church, and notably for the place of the pope therein.

One probably unintended consequence of this shift of focus was a certain tendency to displace the primacy of "communion of life", seen as a "vertical" communion with God and a marked feature of the early book, in favour of communion of life as a "horizontal" relation with other men—albeit one made possible by Trinitarian agency. The creation of a communion (or nondivision) that leaves singularity intact through the nonabsorption of the other is seen by the later Tillard as the divine answer to the problem of human history. Communion with the divine Trinity is cer-

---

[6] Ibid., p. 57.

tainly not effaced in Tillard's later work; despite its concern
with the Church's sacramental structure—above all, liturgical and episcopal—his ecclesiology is far from sociological
in mode. But the mystery of the Trinity, though invoked via
the frequent reference to the Paschal Mystery, from Cross
to Pentecost, loses something of its previous foreground
prominence.

Tillard's "Church of Churches": An Analysis

How, then, does his magnum opus, *Eglise d'églises*, proceed?
I note by way of preamble that Tillard does not devote a
great deal of space to translating his preferred conceptual-
ity into terms of the four marks of the Church—the one,
holy, catholic, and apostolic Church of the Creed—though
he adverts to those marks in interesting ways from time to
time. In his foreword, he explains why that is so. He intends
to explore this article of the Creed not in itself but in its
"root", in its deep source.[7] He is seeking to uncover, we
might say, a basic presupposition of the Creed's makers that
does not come to expression in the four marks, though (we
must presume) it is fully compatible with them.

In the main body of the work, he begins by noting how
hard it is to ascertain any common position about the nature of the Church among the New Testament writers. (It
must be said that the fullest exegetical study of that subject
by a Catholic, Rudolf Schnackenburg's classic *The Church in
the New Testament*, seems to have experienced less difficulty.
But in the generation which separates Schnackenburg from
Tillard, exegetical fashion dictated the evermore determined

---

[7] J. M. R. Tillard, *Eglise d'églises: L'ecclésiologie de communion* (Paris: Cerf,
1987), p. 10.

detection of radical pluralism in the New Testament documents.) However, so Tillard continues, a *theologian*-exegete,
committed to the view that the Holy Spirit has guided the
community Jesus left behind, will take the view that those
basic convictions about the Church that *unfold in the age of
the Fathers*, where things are far clearer, it may be, than in
the New Testament itself, give us access to what the apostolic generation tacitly supposed.[8] And if we survey early
patristic ecclesiology in this spirit, we shall find that the Fathers' vision of the Church is controlled in fact by the New
Testament's presentation of Pentecost.

Taking that as a working hypothesis, then, and looking at
what the event—as understood by Saint Luke in the Book
of Acts—comprises, we can see that Pentecost is "the revelation of communion", the divine disclosure of *koinônia*,
which will be, accordingly, the distinguishing mark of the
Church, as it is of the Last Times inaugurated by the death
and Resurrection of Christ. True, the language of "communion" is not especially apparent in either book of Luke's two-
part work (the Gospel of Luke and the Acts of the Apostles).
There is a rather blatant contrast here with the Johannine
Letters, which fail to describe Pentecost but, by contrast,
have a lot to say about *koinônia*. But perhaps that is not decisive. In line with his general method of reading the New Testament through a patristic lens, Tillard argues that *koinônia*
is of far more importance for apostolic Christianity than the
paucity of Lucan reference might incline us to think.

---

[8] In his *Chair de l'Eglise, chair du Christ: Aux sources de l'ecclésiologie de communion* (Paris: Cerf, 1992), a masterly survey of the biblical and patristic sources
for his ecclesiology, Tillard sought to show that the Fathers of the "undivided
Church" before the 451 Council of Chalcedon (but de facto division begins
twenty years before at Ephesus) had anticipated the basic approach of *Eglise
d'églises*.

The Church-communion begins, then, at Pentecost, when the ecclesial reality first comes into existence as the "mother cell" of the local church of Jerusalem. The account in the Book of Acts, where men of different nations hear the news in their own tongues (cf 2:5–13), makes it plain that the Church founded in this Jerusalem "cell" by the effusion of the Spirit is destined, actually, for all the world. And so Tillard can conclude that *the* Church (the universal Church) and the first local church (the church of Jerusalem) come into existence simultaneously.[9] For Tillard, this simultaneous origin of the universal Church and the local church is what explains how the Church can multiply without dividing, how there can be more and more "churches of God" in different places without there being any less the one single "Church of God".[10]

What by this process comes to be—the creation of the church of Antioch, the church of Corinth, and the rest—is a communion where diversity is integrated into unity and unity expressed as diversity. This is Tillard's version of the marks of unity and catholicity. For him, as for Dulles, and also, if less systematically, for de Lubac, catholicity is primarily diversity rendered harmonious, and so is closely connected to the mark of unity.

The Spirit's outpouring, which reveals the community of the Last Times to be a Church-communion, is inseparable from the apostolic witness whereby the apostles interpreted this Pentecostal theophany in terms of the work

---

[9] Hence his unhappiness about the intervention of John Paul II's Congregation for the Doctrine of the Faith, then presided over by Cardinal Joseph Ratzinger, in its document *On Certain Aspects of the Church Understood as Communion*, which insisted, rather, on the anteriority of the universal Church to the local church.

[10] Tillard, *Eglise d'églises*, p. 29.

and Person of Jesus Christ. The communion of the Church is unthinkable apart from the role of this testimony. Here Tillard draws into his ecclesiology a high theology of the Word, thus extricating himself from the criticism (already made, so he tells us, by one of his teachers at Le Saulchoir) that his thought about the Church was too unilaterally sacramental and, especially, overly Eucharistic.

At the same time, Tillard provides his own version of a theology of the mark of apostolicity. The Church is found in every community where a diverse multitude is integrated into unity, thanks to the reception of the apostolic teaching, notably by Holy Baptism. Here the reference to the baptismal covenant amplifies in a wider sacramental coverage the earlier focus on the Holy Eucharist. It is especially relevant—one might add—to an ecumenical context, where not all the "ecclesial communities" engaged in bilateral dialogue with the (Roman) Catholic Church have, from the viewpoint of that Church (owing to lack of the apostolic succession), an assured Eucharistic life.

So far, one might have the impression that this is almost entirely a pneumatic ecclesiology, in the sense of an ecclesiology worked out in terms of the economy of the Holy Spirit, with the work of Christ largely consigned to the task of explaining how it was the Spirit came, at the first Pentecost, to be poured out. But the same patristic authors who identify Pentecost as the beginning of the Church also insist on the equally essential Christological dimension. Undergirding the Church is a relation to Jesus Christ: a relation best thought of as that of a body to its head. Tillard makes also this aspect of the Fathers' thought his own, and, accordingly, his ecclesiology is not only a Spirit ecclesiology but also, and very much so, a theology of the Body of Christ.

This it must be if Tillard is to reintegrate into this account that passionate interest in the sacrament of the Lord's Body and Blood, which was at the centre of his earlier, more exclusively Eucharistic, ecclesiology. "In the personal body of Christ, the body in which the drama of pardon and reconciliation was lived out, is the true 'meeting-point' of the new humanity, the precise spot where the *koinônia* (which Paul describes as a body) finds itself constituted and present, already all there in its very principle."[11] Following the Letter to the Ephesians, Tillard argues it is the Resurrection of that torn yet immaculate Body that seals the "return to unity" (the Ephesian term would be *recapitulation*) of mankind, now (in principle) made one again.

From here, the move back to the Eucharist is relatively plain sailing. Since the Eucharistic Body is truly the Body of *this* Lord—the One who is the principle of unity for redeemed mankind—each Eucharistic celebration brings us into communion with the whole Church. Indeed, "the universal Church is immanent in the local church in communion with the Eucharistic body".[12] So the identity of the one Church with the first local church, the mother cell of Jerusalem, which Tillard earlier established on pneumatological grounds, may now be extended. The one Church is identical with every local church, not only by reference to pneumatological consideration of what happened at the first Pentecost but also on Christological grounds, owing to the Eucharistic celebration in multiple places of the one Body of Christ.

And this is where Tillard's version of the mark of holiness

[11] Ibid., p. 41.
[12] Ibid., p. 44.

is located. For him, the Church is holy owing to her inser-
tion through the Eucharist into the personal reality of Jesus
Christ. In the Eucharist, communion is bestowed as "the
fructification of the gift of salvation present in the Body and
Blood of the Lord".[13] And, he enquires rhetorically, what
is this if not the gift of holiness? It is in the Eucharistic celebration that the Church is in all reality "holy Church". It
is in the Mass that the mark of holiness found in the Creed
is realised. Tillard notes, perfectly correctly, that both the
Eucharist and the Church can be called *communio sanctorum*,
and this term signifies for him "the depths of *koinônia*, a
koinônia in the single witness given since Pentecost . . . to
the Gospel of God which triumphs in the Resurrection of
the Crucified".[14]

Tillard admits that a Eucharistic ecclesiology—or even, at
the wrong hands, an ecclesiology of communion—is weak
in showing how the Church is by her nature missionary,
that dimension of her being more customarily reflected in
a theology of "quantitative" catholicity. In *Eglise d'églises*,
he sought to correct the lack of missionary thrust in his
earlier, purer version of such ecclesiology. When through
the Eucharist the ecclesial Body of Christ is conjoined with
Christ's personal Body, the Church making Eucharist tacitly commits herself to everything implied in Christ's Lordship over the universe. In that "everything", so Tillard now
insists, missionary expansion is the chief thing to be mentioned.[15] And even for those who do not find themselves at
the *synaxis* of an "authentic" Eucharist, missionary service,
along with martyrdom, and the offering of prayer and in-

[13] Ibid., p. 50.
[14] Ibid., p. 45.
[15] Ibid., pp. 45–46.

tercession, should count as significant "zones" surrounding the true nucleus of communion, the Eucharistic Liturgy, where the Church of God is all that she is called to be.[16]

The Visible Structure of the Church

But surely the mandating of mission should not be severed from the sacramental event where communion is most truly itself? This brings us to the question of the visible—and not least the ministerial and thus governmental—structure of the Church. Every community that celebrates the authentic Eucharist (in an ecumenical context, courtesy may lead to bracketing out the question of just what an authentic Eucharist might be) can count as an example of *koinônia*, of communion. To begin with, in each city there was only one Eucharistic assembly, under the bishop. Today, many assemblies gather under their presbyters, ordained and appointed by the bishop. That makes the local church a communion of communions: a communion of Eucharistic communities, all of which are in communion with one bishop.

By appeal to the same reasoning, the Church throughout the world—the Church that celebrates the authentic Eucharist, be it noted—must be accounted a communion of such wider communions, with each of the latter having its bishop at its centre. And so—and here we get a very ungainly formula when one spells it out—we have in the universal Church an episcopally ordered communion-of-communions-of-communions. If this sounds like an ecclesiastical technician speaking, I should add that Tillard does

[16] Ibid., pp. 60–66.

not fail to emphasise the spiritual and moral charge *koinônia* carries when considered in its aspect of relation to God. It signifies—so he interprets the proclamation of reconciliation found in the Letter to the Ephesians (2:13–22)—"grace received and glory to be spread abroad, victory over hate and charity to proclaim".[17]

What Tillard has now to show is that everything that belongs to the accredited pattern of Catholic ecclesiology can be situated within this frame. After all, there are other concepts in Catholic ecclesiology, with quite as good a New Testament pedigree, which seem on the face of it to lend themselves better to a more "universalist" ecclesiology where the particular churches make their appearance as "portions" or "parts" of a whole. "People of God" would seem an obvious example, and so would the image of the Church as a "spiritual house". As it happens, precisely these two motifs, in their occurrence in Saint Augustine's writings, had been treated by Tillard's exact contemporary, the youthful Joseph Ratzinger (both men were born in 1927).[18] In a lengthy section of *Eglise d'églises*, Tillard, it is true, has recourse to the imagery of the People of God—necessary for him, so that his account of a "Church of churches" be not hopelessly overloaded with concern for bishops rather than those they serve. But he fills out that imagery with the distinctive conceptual content of the ecclesiology of communion.[19] Evidently, this was a markedly different kind of patristic *ressourcement* from Ratzinger's—one more indebted

---

[17] Ibid., p. 71. This thought finds its further development in the beautiful section on the Church as "minister of salvation", pp. 291–318.

[18] J. Ratzinger, *Volk und Haus Gottes in Augustins Lehre von der Kirche* (Munich: Zink, 1954).

[19] Tillard, *Eglise d'eglises*, pp. 113–85.

to Eastern sources—where ecclesiological doctrine is concerned.[20]

Eglise d'églises closes with lengthy discussions of the visible communion of the churches,[21] along with, at the service of communion, the lives of the ordained.[22] It may seem surprising that Tillard discusses the ministry before he treats the communion of churches—just as (so we shall see) a Neo-Scholastic ecclesiologist like Charles Journet discusses the apostolic hierarchy before treating any other aspect of the Church. Journet's reasons are largely pedagogical; Tillard, by contrast, is following the logic of his starting point: the Eucharistic synaxis of a particular church, gathering all sorts and conditions of men under its episcopal head, and acting in its own place as *the* expression of the communion of men with God in Christ, the manifestation of the *Catholica*.[23] This high doctrine of the local church—assembled around its bishop who, entrusted with the task of preserving it in the Tradition, celebrates these mysteries—will be even more apparent in his last major work, *L'Eglise locale*, significantly, an even heftier tome than *Eglise d'églises* itself.[24] It is in that book that Tillard produces the extraordinary maxim—extraordinary even for someone for whom catholicity is primarily qualitative in character—"catholic *because* local".[25] His defence is not unpersuasive: the Church exhibits her catholicity by

---

[20] In *Chair de l'Eglise, chair du Christ*, his patristic apologia, Tillard gives special emphasis to one Western Father, Augustine, but two Easterners, Chrysostom and Cyril of Alexandria.

[21] Tillard, *Eglise d'eglises*, pp. 323–97.

[22] Ibid., pp. 217–321.

[23] Ibid., pp. 220–24.

[24] J. M. R. Tillard, *L'Eglise locale: Ecclésiologie de communion et catholicité* (Paris: Cerf, 1995).

[25] Ibid., p. 125; italics are added.

the way the churches that form her communion, each in its own place, take up the culture of the spot, hallow what in it is capable of (metaphorical) baptism, and throw it open —in communion with each other—to the full dimensions of the *Catholica*. Each local church should be considered as "the fruit of the *katholou* [wholeness] of the Gospel of God in the *totality* of the *place*—at once geographical, cultural, historical, sociological—where a human community lives out its destiny."[26]

Inspired by the relation between *surnaturel* and *charnel* in the writing of the early-twentieth-century French poet and publicist Charles Péguy, Tillard pressed into service both patristic scholarship and his long experience of ecumenical discussion (above all, with the Orthodox), producing en route a profound theology of the laity (the baptised) and of the three orders of bishops, presbyters, deacons.

Questions—Not Least about the Bishop of Rome

But how on earth, we might ask, can Tillard's approach, strongly localist (though not Congregationalist) as it is,[27] cope with such doctrinal claims as the following: the Mystical Body of Christ subsists in the (Roman) Catholic Church; the episcopate constitutes a single unitary college; the pope is the supreme pastor of the universal Church; an ecumenical council or even the pope himself is infallible? All of these assume (with de Lubac) that the Church is a mystery expressed as a society with a corporate identity expressed

[26] Ibid., p. 53; italics are original.
[27] The local church, for Tillard, is always found "within the *synergia* [collaboration] of the 'catholica ecclesia Dei'", ibid., p. 387, a phrase title which governs the enormous chapter that runs from p. 387 to p. 552 of this work.

through a unitary hierarchy and presenting herself as our common Mother. These are notions typical of an ecclesiology that thinks chiefly in terms of the one Church not the many churches—even if Tillard would insist that he *can* do justice to the one Church as when he writes of the local church:

> It must live in and for the truth of its Eucharist. Let it be what it receives, as Augustine would say. And since what it receives is the Body of the Reconciliation, of the universal *koinônia*, of the *Catholica*, it has to live with the "care for all the churches"—let us understand that as "the communion of all the baptised"—in the grace of the Spirit of the Risen One.[28]

Tillard is by no means at a loss before the questions supporters of a universalist ecclesiology would pose. Thus, for instance, as to the famous eighth paragraph of *Lumen gentium*, where the Mystical Body is said to "subsist in" the (Roman) Catholic Church, for Tillard the "Church of God" subsists in the "communion of communions" that is in full communion with the See of Rome in the sense that God's Church enjoys there a greater "fullness" and "force" of manifestation than in other such "communions", whether these be, as with the Orthodox, "churches" in the complete sense (with an authentic Eucharist, i.e., one celebrated in the apostolic succession) or simply "ecclesial communities" (whose participation in apostolic tradition is deficient in this respect).[29] Or again, he can ask his readers, rhetorically, what is the solidarity of bishops whose churches are all manifestations of the one Church if not a "college"—in the preferred term of

---

[28] Tillard, *Eglise d'églises*, p. 283.

[29] Ibid., pp. 393–96: not a very satisfactory discussion, it must be said, since the terms *fullness* and *force*, borrowed from the Louvain theologian Gerard Philips, are inadequately defined.

the universalist ecclesiology, which is more at home in the official documents of Catholicism.[30] And if we are anxious that, in a "Church of churches", we might lose the sense of the one Church as our Mother, Tillard would reassure us: the Church manifested in the churches is the Bride of Christ, as the Letter to the Ephesians has it, thus she must also be, as the Fathers often insist, *Ecclesia Mater*.[31] No actual theological argument is offered there, it seems, so as to make the language of Scripture and the Fathers more perspicuous in, specifically, an ecclesiology of communion. Yet Tillard's desire to avoid a form of Eucharistic ecclesiology that could seriously undermine the Catholic concept of the one universal Church is palpable.

> The deep communion which the Eucharist—and it alone —accomplishes only emerges in visible form when those who preside at the synaxis everywhere in the world and who have so presided ever since Pentecost, as the icon of Christ "gathering into one" the people of God, are themselves bound together in a single ministerial body.[32]

In this context, the *question of the bishop of Rome* (to which, after this statement, Tillard immediately passes) is a significant example of how an ecclesiology of communion sees things, and it has the advantage of being one of Tillard's favourites. In his book-length study of the place of the pope in the Church, Tillard worked out an attractive vocabulary for the role of the Roman bishop, whom he presents, in the light of patristic texts about the see of the apostles Peter and Paul, as "the sentinel, the 'watcher', the memory of the apostolic faith, above all, with his brother bishops, so as to

[30] Ibid., pp. 251–68.
[31] Ibid., pp. 202–3, and especially the extensive note 165.
[32] Ibid., p. 323.

keep them in fidelity to their mission and especially to open them unceasingly to the universal dimensions of salvation and of the Church of God".[33]

But, despite the occasional use of "communion" language at the First Vatican Council, the affirmation of the pope's universal jurisdiction and infallibility in defining dogma was arrived at, like the other traditional theses of Western Catholic theology mentioned above, not so much in terms of an ecclesiology of communion, but rather within the limits of a more straightforward theology of the universal Church. When the pope is presented as the "servant of communion" (Tillard's preferred title) or again as the *centrum communionis* (a phrase Tillard borrowed from the aula discussion at the First Vatican Council), his task as universal pastor and, in *ex cathedra* judgments, universal doctor of all Christians has to be reexpressed in novel ways.

Tillard succeeds in showing how it is possible for an ecclesiology of communion to make sense of these claims— possible, but somewhat difficult and entailing a rather convoluted process of argumentation, whose single most crucial idea, where the teaching office is concerned, is the concept of "recognition" or "reception".

By a process of sifting, followed by a discriminating acceptance (or alternatively, rejection) of what is done and believed in various local churches, the communion of communions (*Eglise d'eglises*) can adopt a united position and take action as a whole. In this, the concert of bishops, who are guardians of the unity of their individual churches, plays a vital role, as does the bishop of Rome as guardian of the unity of the concert of bishops. The role of the concert of bishops and, within that, of the bishop of Rome is to mediate

[33] J. M. R. Tillard, *L'Evêque de Rome* (Paris: Cerf, 1982), p. 72.

the relations of the churches and to test the claim that some interpretation of the faith or way of practicing it is (or is not) in keeping with the Tradition entrusted to each cell of the Church, when in the Holy Spirit each local church accepted by Baptism the apostolic witness to Christ and began to live from the resources of the Eucharist where both local bishop and pope are commemorated.[34]

As to the pastoral or governing office (where the question at stake, for the Roman bishop, is not infallibility but universal jurisdiction), that for Tillard is supremely (and ordinarily) expressed by the way the pope "situates" and "orientates" a newly ordained bishop within the communion of bishops and thus of the local churches at large.[35] This the pope does through the "canonical determination" (to this or that charge in the Church), which follows on the new bishop's ordination. That ordination is itself an act accomplished by the Holy Spirit at the hands of bishops from other local churches, whereas the role of the bishop of Rome (who, as Tillard envisages matters, will not have actually *appointed* the candidate) is to enable the new bearer of *episkopê* to enter with full recognition on an appropriate range of ministerial services in the wider communion of the churches. After that, the pope will, basically, leave him alone to get on with the business of being the high priest, shepherd, and teacher of his church.

Tillard also envisages rather rare, out-of-the-ordinary cases in which a bishop of Rome, faced with some grave threat to the unity of faith and practice, might appropriately intervene in the affairs of others so as to "safeguard the communion of

---

[34] On the (doctrinally delicate but ecumenically crucial) issue of reception, see Tillard, *Eglise d'églises*, pp. 155–81.

[35] Tillard, *L'Evêque de Rome*, p. 193.

the churches".[36] This would be, however, in "synergy"—collaboration—with the occupants of other major sees and acting on the principle of subsidiarity, meaning that nothing would be done at a higher level unless it could not be done at a lower one[37] and that nothing would be done at a higher level unless it was proposed by way of response to "fraternal" invitation.[38]

Conclusion on Tillard

There is little doubt that Tillard's distinctive approach to the mystery of the Church appeals to sympathetic Orthodox (and to patristically inclined Anglicans, especially if they are "Orthodoxophile"). His ecumenical partnership with John Zizioulas (who shares, from the Orthodox angle, much of Tillard's ecclesial vision)[39] has been of huge value for the bilateral dialogue between Constantinople (and her sister churches) and Rome. Given the great importance of reunion with the separated East (not least to counterbalance certain Protestantising tendencies in the contemporary Catholic West), Tillard merits his place among the masters of ecclesiology. And yet his notion of the Church as communion has to bear the weight of a tradition for which the Mystical Body of Christ subsists in the (Roman) Catholic Church in a way that permits that same Church to teach *definitively* about human salvation and to claim for her

[36] Ibid., pp. 220–35.
[37] Ibid., p. 233.
[38] Ibid., p. 227.
[39] J. Fontbona i Missé, *Comunión y sinodalidad. La ecclesiología eucaristica después de N. Afanasiev en I. Zizioulas y J. M. R. Tillard* (Barcelona: Editorial Herder, 1994).

pastoral mission a divine mandate to gather all nations *unreservedly* into one.

Tillard could sometimes speak as if that key verb *subsists* should be taken in a provisional sense, as though the real subsisting were still to come, in an ecumenically more complete future.[40] On an eschatological reading of the marks of the Church, flagged up in the opening paragraphs of *Figuring Out the Church*, it is certainly legitimate to point to the unfinished character of the Church's present condition. Our account of the mark of holiness has already accepted as much. But, for a Catholic theologian, such provisionality will never be carried to the point where the Church of the present is deemed disabled from carrying out essential functions such as the definition of doctrine or legitimate missionary expansion throughout the planet—so deemed owing to the alleged insufficiencies of her ontology: her being one, holy, catholic, and apostolic, *now*. Indeed Tillard draws back from such conclusions. But the conceptual scheme he urges on us (for reasons of fidelity to the patristic epoch and *rapprochement* with the contemporary Orthodox) does not make it easy for us to speak of "the Church" teaching, or otherwise acting with authority, as a unitary whole.

In Chapter 1 of this book, we saw reasons for thinking that the unity of the Church is, in the last analysis, a more pressing consideration than is her multiplicity or plurality, and we returned to the theme in Chapter 4. There is indeed an obvious sense in which the Church is composed of local communities (and she would look very odd without them). Yet that is not, in Congar's word, the "decisive" consideration in ecclesiology.[41] As he put it, persons are "converted

---

[40] Tillard, *Eglise d'eglises*, p. 29.
[41] Y. Congar, "Théologie de l'Eglise particulière", in *Mission sans frontières*, ed. A. M. Henry (Paris: Cerf, 1962), pp. 17–52.

and incorporated" into a Church that is "transcendent . . . in relation to earthly categories and particularities".[42] Does that mean that we are uninterested in the way local churches can usher the human riches of specific cultures into the unity of the *Catholica* of the Creed? Not at all. It was in Chapter 4 above that we saw how Dulles could furnish a maximally rich doctrine of catholicity without surrendering the primacy of unity. And we must not exaggerate Tillard's own account of the plural character of the Church. In his own warning words: "Pluralism ceases to be in harmony with the very nature of the Church when it ceases to be founded on a unity of faith, of sacramental life, and of mission."[43] Shall we find assistance for any infelicities there may be in his thought if we move for the last pair of portraits in this study from the French to the Swiss? We shall certainly find more of a sense of the Church as a total theological person.

[42] Ibid.
[43] Tillard, *Eglise d'églises*, p. 327.

7

HANS URS VON BALTHASAR

Balthasar's Life

Hans Urs von Balthasar is probably the best-known modern Catholic theologian, having overtaken Karl Rahner in the theological Grand National—or, rather, International, if the output of learned studies is any guide.[1] He was born in 1905 to a patrician Catholic family in Lucerne, in central Switzerland.[2] As an adolescent and young adult, he proved to be highly gifted artistically as well as formidably intelligent. After studies in various universities, he received a doctorate in 1928 for a huge and unmanageable thesis about the religious implications of German literature and philosophy: what his Protestant contemporary Paul Tillich would have called their "ultimate concerns".[3] The following year he entered the Jesuits just at the time when various brilliant members of the Society were launching the movement of patristic *ressourcement* and opening to a wider intellectual and

[1] The best overall study of his thought, probably in any language, is E. T. Oakes [S.J.], *Pattern of Redemption. The Theology of Hans Urs von Balthasar* (New York: Continuum, 1994).

[2] For a fuller vignette of his life and work, see A. Nichols, O.P., "An Introduction to Balthasar", in Nichols, *The Word Has Been Abroad: A Guide through Balthasar's Aesthetics* (Edinburgh: T. & T. Clark, 1998), pp. ix–xx.

[3] H. U. von Balthasar, *Apokalypse der deutschen Seele* (Salzburg: Pustet, 1937–1939). This three-volume work was republished at Einsiedeln in 1998.

spiritual world known as *la nouvelle théologie*. We have seen how Henri de Lubac was among their number.

After ordination to the priesthood, Balthasar opted to become a student chaplain in Basel rather than a lecturer at the Gregorian University in Rome. In the Providence of God, this made it possible for him to meet Adrienne von Speyr, whom he instructed and received into the Catholic Church, whose spiritual adviser he became, and whose mystical effusions he recorded and edited.[4] With von Speyr, Balthasar believed himself called to found a Secular Institute, of which she would be the spiritual mother and he the fatherly theologian and guide. Quite apart from anxieties about the content of von Speyr's visionary experience, this went against the traditional Jesuit rejection of any form of sisterhoods, oblateships, or third orders as quasi-constituent parts of the Society. Balthasar was obliged to choose between it and the budding *Johannesgemeinschaft* or Community of John.

His leaving the Society, and doing so in those circumstances, made him if not quite a pariah, then rather an uncertain figure so far as official Catholicism was concerned. It explains his failure to find in the mailbox one of those invitations to the Second Vatican Council that Rahner, de Lubac, Tillard, and many others received. He seems not to have regretted this, and he used his time profitably for writing instead. Indeed, the story of his writing takes up in effect the rest of his life, when little else happened except his being named a cardinal by John Paul II in 1988 and dying three days before he could be given the cardinal's hat, which should have been conferred on 29 June of that year.

---

[4] H. U. von Balthasar, *First Glance at Adrienne von Speyr* (San Francisco: Ignatius Press, 1981).

Balthasar's Work

Balthasar's principal theological offering to posterity is his trilogy, consisting of a theological aesthetics, a theological dramatics, and a theological logic.[5] The idea behind the trilogy is taken from Christian Scholasticism. According to the latter (at any rate, in many of its representatives), being—the being of whatever is—is transcendentally characterised as beautiful, good, and true. This means that over and above, not simply in and through, the qualities that warrant any of the more particular things we might wish to say about X (whether X be amoeba or wombat or archangel), X can always be described as in its own way beautiful, good, and true—true, namely, to the creative idea of it in the mind of God. We live in a world that in these three modes reflects the divine perfection, the perfection of its Creator. In the trilogy, Balthasar works out this theme in relation to revelation and salvation, showing how these constitute the most powerful beauty man has known (the aesthetics), the most helpful of all goods man has ever known (the dramatics), and the most comprehensive truth (the logic).

In the aesthetics,[6] theology takes its departure point from the mystery of revelation made known in the incarnate and crucified Word of God. In him is manifested a glory or splendour that integrates all natural beauty and surpasses all human attempts to order the world. In the dramatics,[7] Balthasar further explores the drama of the Incarnation and Atonement

[5] For a brief introduction, see A. Nichols, O.P., *A Key to Balthasar: Hans Urs von Balthasar on Beauty, Goodness and Truth* (London: Darton, Longman, and Todd, 2011).

[6] H. U. von Balthasar, *The Glory of the Lord: A Theological Aesthetics*, 7 vols. (San Francisco: Ignatius Press, 1982–1991).

[7] H. U. von Balthasar, *Theo-drama: Theological Dramatic Theory*, 5 vols. (San Francisco: Ignatius Press, 1988–1998).

as the action through which God seeks to gather together and bring home everything worthwhile in creation. In the logic,[8] he shows how the inner logic of God's action in history is disclosed in Jesus Christ through the Holy Spirit, the Interpreter of Christ, as a truth greater than any truth that can be conceived. Seen theologically, then, the beautiful is divine Glory in which men are called to share; the good is merciful love by which they hope for salvation; the true is the Word of the Father, communicated by the Spirit, through whom they know the love that is beyond understanding. The transcendentals are theologically transmuted without, however, losing their philosophical identity in the process.

In the course of the trilogy, Balthasar has a certain amount to say about ecclesiology. Especially is this so in the opening volume of the aesthetics, where he considers the Church as the community that perceives the beauty of Christ and responds to it, and in the closing volume of the logic, where, in looking at the truth of the Holy Spirit, Balthasar ponders how the Spirit makes known his truth in the Church both in subjective ways, through personal experience and notably the charism-borne missions of saints and mystics, and also in objective ways, through Scripture, Tradition (including the Liturgy), and Church office (the magisterium).

But in scanning his ecclesiology, we are not confined to these sources since the trilogy, while his most important legacy, is by no means the whole of what he bequeathed to us.

His other theological writings are less easily described in the odd, well-chosen compendious phrase, though what he

---

[8] H. U. von Balthasar, *Theo-logic: Theological Logical Theory*, 3 vols. (San Francisco: Ignatius Press, 2000–2005).

was trying to do is clear enough.[9] It was to salvage enough of the best divinity, spirituality, and literature of past and present to ensure that at least among his readers (and readers of other works put out by his publishing house), there would be passed on to posterity a Catholic culture, wide enough and rich enough to serve as a basis for Christian life and mission as it ought to be rather than as it often is.

Not surprisingly, then, one can turn up major ecclesiological discussions in all sorts of places in Balthasar's highly diverse oeuvre. Of special relevance to our topic are, for example, the essay collection called *Spouse of the Word*;[10] his polemical book against modern-day detractors of the papacy, *The Office of Peter and the Structure of the Church* (a better if less punchy title than the original, *The Anti-Roman Affect*);[11] and a study of the French novelist and essayist Georges Bernanos, called in the German original *The Lived Church* (*Gelebte Kirche*).[12]

The Origin of Church
in the Kenosis of Christ

In his glowing account of the events of the Easter Triduum, *Mysterium Paschale*, Balthasar accepts the patristic thesis that the Church is born from the opened side of Christ on the

[9] A. Nichols, O.P., *Divine Fruitfulness: A Guide through Balthasar's Theology beyond the Trilogy* (Edinburgh: T. & T. Clark, 2007).

[10] H. U. von Balthasar, *Explorations in Theology*, vol. 2: *Spouse of the Word* (San Francisco: Ignatius Press, 1991).

[11] H. U. von Balthasar, *The Office of Peter and the Structure of the Church* (San Francisco: Ignatius Press, 1986).

[12] H. U. von Balthasar, *Bernanos: An Ecclesial Existence* (San Francisco: Ignatius Press, 1996).

Cross.[13] From the riven side of the Lord asleep in death, while the blood and water, symbolic of the saving sacraments, flowed forth, the Church took her birth—just as Eve, in the Genesis creation narrative, had likewise been "born" from the side of the sleeping Adam.

His own explanation of this mysterious development runs as follows. At the Crucifixion, the people of the Covenant —the old Israel—was "wholly recreated out of the single, fully valid Representative of that Covenant on earth", Jesus Christ, the new Adam, as he lay asleep in death.[14] This statement provides the grounding for a hymn to charity or, if you prefer, a charter for nuptial mysticism. "Born of the utmost love of God for the world, the Church herself is essentially love."[15] To substantiate that statement about the Church's being, Balthasar makes much of the New Eve: the Mother of the Lord, who gives her loving "bridal" consent to all her Son was doing at the Cross.[16] We shall see in a moment how despite robustly acknowledging the "directly masculine and hierarchical aspect of the Church's foundation",[17] Balthasar nonetheless regards the Church as more fundamentally Marian—and, therefore, feminine—in character.

But the Church the Son brings into being for the Father's glory in the events of Easter is a Church *of the Holy Spirit*.

Although much in the founding of the Church was prepared in the time before Easter—in the disciples' training in discipleship and their instruction—the real act of

[13] H. U. von Balthasar, *Mysterium Paschale: The Mystery of Easter* (San Francisco: Ignatius Press, 2000), p. 132.

[14] Ibid.

[15] Ibid., p. 134.

[16] Ibid., p. 136.

[17] Ibid., p. 256.

founding could not take place until the Risen One had completed his own work, and, in the power of his death and Resurrection, could breathe out his Spirit upon the Church-in-the-founding.[18]

The Church, become alive at Pentecost, will be henceforth "the work and the dwelling place of the Third Divine Person, the Holy Spirit".[19] That the saving sign which is the Church is fully constituted in the moment of Pentecost perhaps explains Balthasar's very strong preference for qualitative, over against quantitative, catholicity.[20] In many situations, the Church seems peripheral—but then everything in the world is peripheral in relation to the *true* centre, the Holy Eucharist, where "the Risen One . . . no longer reins in his self-outpouring but in the Eucharist perseveres in a love that 'goes to the end'".[21]

Balthasar's evident intention to bind ecclesiology as firmly as possible to the Paschal Mystery, above all to Pentecost (and not least in relation to the Eucharistic celebration),[22] has a certain affinity with Tillard's approach to the Church —though Balthasar is much more willing to allow ecclesiological thinking to take off from the biblical data, rather

---

[18] Ibid., p. 255.

[19] Balthasar, "Charis and charisma", in *Spouse of the Word*, p. 301.

[20] In view of the Church's real dimensions, "all that remains as a possible claim is simply a claim to a *qualitative* catholicity, one that can speak to every other potency in the world", H. U. von Balthasar, "The Claim to Catholicity", in *Explorations in Theology*, vol. 4: *Spirit and Institution* (San Francisco: Ignatius Press, 1995), pp. 65–121, here at p. 67; italics original.

[21] Ibid., p. 110, with an internal quotation of Jn 13:1.

[22] Setting this theme in the widest possible context is the coauthored essay by N. Healy and D. L. Schindler, "For the Life of the World: Hans Urs von Balthasar on the Church as Eucharist", in *The Cambridge Companion to Hans Urs von Balthasar*, ed. E. T. Oakes, S.J., and D. Moss (Cambridge: Cambridge University Press, 2004), pp. 51–63.

than to move constantly in their ambit. Typically, for example, he explains the Pentecost event by arguing that it is when the Son undergoes Incarnation to the uttermost, in the final sufferings on the Tree of the Cross, that the Holy Spirit most completely penetrates his manhood and enables it to become the principle of a new, engraced humanity in the Church.[23]

For this reason, I note, Balthasar was very opposed to any counterposition of the words *spiritual* and *incarnational*. The flesh that is (in Tertullian's word) the "hinge", the crucial factor, in our salvation, is not to be set over against the spiritual life, the pneumatic life, the life the Holy Spirit gives. This has consequences for ecclesiology. No church that would be exclusively spiritual and subjective and not at all corporeal and objective in its manner of proceeding could possibly be the continuing Spirit-carried presence of Jesus Christ.

The Church of the Spirit—Objectively, Subjectively

The last volume of the trilogy has much along these lines. The Spirit who pours forth at Pentecost is not only the personal love of the Father and the Son, the Expression of their inter-subjectivity. He is also supremely objective, the Fruit of their love. This duality has ecclesiological implications if it is by the Spirit that the Church born on Good Friday is manifested at Pentecost.

In the Church, the Spirit shows himself as both totally subjective and totally objective. In the first respect, he is the Person who inspires sanctity in human subjects, initiating

[23] H. U. von Balthasar, *Theologik*, vol. 3: *Der Geist der Wahrheit* (Johannesverlag: Einsiedeln, 1997), p. 176.

prayer, stimulating repentance and reconciliation, granting people mystical and other charismatic gifts, as well as giving individuals the capacity to bear witness to Christ.[24] All of that—"subjective Spirit" Balthasar calls it, in a play of words and concepts drawn from Hegel's phenomenology (and more specifically, Hegel's account of the growth of freedom in civil society)—the Holy Spirit most certainly is.

But then there is also the second respect: the Spirit as "objective" in the Church. For the Spirit also inspires outer forms and institutional mediations of the saving revelation. Examples are Tradition and Scripture, Church office and preaching, the Liturgy and the sacraments, and even canon law and theology.[25] All of this—"objective Spirit"—is also he. On the basis of Christ's founding activity, what the Holy Spirit builds up in the Church institution is quite as much his own personal work—the work of the One who is Expression and Fruit of the love of Father and Son—as is the personal holiness that the pattern of the Church's life makes possible. So we can say that Balthasar writes a promystical ecclesiology, which is also, and equally, an anti-Gnostic one.

In his study of Bernanos, for example, he praises the novelist for realizing that the saint—

> the subjective following of Christ and the realization of [Christ's] holiness within the sphere of the human person—is simply unthinkable without the objective holiness of the Church, of her official ministry and of her sacraments. . . . This is the exact point where Bernanos' saintly heroes begin to emerge.[26]

But what that in turn means is (to continue the quotation) that "the whole of the hierarchical and sacramental order

[24] Ibid., pp. 340–80.
[25] Ibid., pp. 294–339.
[26] Balthasar, *Bernanos*, p. 260.

in the end is there for the saint, that is, for the subjective sanctification of Christians in general, for those who *au fond* have already been made holy through baptism."[27]

This emphasis on the way objective holiness (objective Spirit) is there for the sake of subjective holiness (subjective Spirit)—which itself requires its objective counterpart for its realisation—enables Balthasar to give a very well-rounded portrait of the Church, omitting no important element. Everything, from mystical grace to canon law, is provided with a theological interpretation within a comprehensive view of the place of the Church in the economy of the Holy Spirit. But above all, the two poles of holiness, objective and subjective, are summed up in the priest (who expresses the objectivity of the Word and sacraments) and the saint (who is their fruit). Portraying that is what he finds so admirable in Bernanos' Catholic novels. "[T]he ecclesial drama is played out between the priest and the saint."[28]

The Church as the Subject of Christian Experience

When investigating de Lubac's ecclesiology, we finished by considering the way he invokes the Church in his book on the structure of the Apostles' Creed. There de Lubac explained how the best way to avoid either exaggerating or minimising the place of the Church in the corpus of Christian doctrine as a whole is to consider her as the true subject of the word *credo*. She is the corporate subject who carries out the activity of believing to which the Creed attests. As individual Christians, we believe by participating in the Church's own primordial act of faith. The more we grow in

[27] Ibid.
[28] Ibid., p. 263.

the life of faith, the more we are in fact—whether we realize this or not—deepening our appropriation of *her* faith.

Balthasar takes this idea further. He agrees with de Lubac that the Church is the primordial subject of believing. But he asks a further question, about how the fundamental (he calls it "archetypal") Christian experience comes to be constituted in the apostolic generation and transmitted—by participation—in all the generations that follow. In sharing the faith of the Church, we participate in the Church's archetypal experience of salvation through Jesus Christ. But how?

In the opening volume of his theological aesthetics, Balthasar proposes that the Church receives from the apostolic generation a fourfold tradition of archetypal experience: fourfold because it is Petrine, Pauline, Johannine, and Marian.[29] With Peter, Paul, John, and Mary are associated characteristic expressions of the new mode of grace given in Christian origins, in the moment of the Incarnation. Continually made present to believers, this experience of the key figures of the Dominical or apostolic generation goes on nourishing the Church's members over time. Their archetypal experience shapes our experience of the Church—when, that is, we allow our experience to be maximally full or, as Balthasar would say, maximally Catholic: a word he uses not just to indicate the claim to catholicity made in the Creed but also to denote, as it more commonly does in everyday speech, what is distinctive about the Church (Tillard would prefer to say "the churches") in communion with the See of Rome.

In brief, what Balthasar says about these coconstituting inputs into archetypal apostolic experience runs like this. The

---

[29] H. U. von Balthasar, *The Glory of the Lord: A Theological Aesthetics*, vol. 1: *Seeing the Form* (San Francisco: Ignatius Press, 1982), pp. 350–65.

Petrine contribution consisted of the apostolic preaching and the sacraments, which are its follow-up. And through the hierarchy, the apostolic succession of teachers and celebrants of sacraments continues in the later Church. The *Pauline* contribution consisted of charismatic and visionary graces, which, however, are not given simply for the enjoyment (if that is the word) of individuals. As we see from Saint Paul's Damascus road experience, such graces generate missions (very much in the plural) that serve the overall mission (in the singular) of the Church. The *Johannine* contribution consists of contemplative love, so notable in the Fourth Gospel and the Letters, and the impetus to move forward to the heavenly Jerusalem, typical of the Johannine Revelation. The *Marian* archetype, which, as we shall see in a moment, is the most important of the four, enables us to experience the bodily, tangible life of the Church with her sacraments and institutions (the Petrine contribution) as the means for the spiritual experience of Christ and thus of God. Just so the virginal body of Mary was the means for the Incarnation of the uncreated Word.

All these are, for Balthasar, archetypal experiences, originally enjoyed by this fourfold of figures in the Dominical or apostolic generation. They are called archetypal not just because they happened at the start of the Church's life. Balthasar is not just saying they are early influences on the Church, which, though true, would be merely a commonplace. He is also saying that they form the lives of Christians considered precisely as believers, the "life-form of believing man".[30]

---

[30] Ibid., p. 364.

The Operation of the Petrine,
Johannine, and Marian Principles

Elsewhere Balthasar treats of these constituent features of Christian subjectivity *in* the Church as constituent principles of the Christian objectivity *of* the Church, principles that give the Church her basic structure.[31] In this context (as reflected in my subtitle for this section), the Pauline element tends to disappear. This is not because Balthasar was uncertain as to whether to regard it as important. Unusual charisms and mystical graces are extremely important to him, not only because Adrienne von Speyr constantly presented him with a dramatic living example, but also because he saw them as the driving force behind the missions of many saints. Whereas some saints became saints through living in heroic fashion the ordinary Christian life, others were raised up by God so as to launch new missions in the Church: new forms of spirituality, new kinds of service.[32] Of course, Balthasar was also aware of more everyday charisms, whether attached to office or simply to the royal and universal priesthood of the baptized, "differentiations" (he would have said) of the grace of redeemed existence.[33] Such "ordinary" charisms are described by Paul, but they are not embodied in him, for if anyone's life and mission was extraordinary in the Church it was his. The point about this Pauline element is that, just because it is a matter of exceptional vocations, it does not belong, for Balthasar, to describing the *basic* structure of the

[31] Texts on this topic from a variety of Balthasar's writings are skillfully woven together in J. Saward, *The Mysteries of March: Hans Urs von Balthasar on the Incarnation and Easter* (London: Collins, 1990), pp. 77–81.

[32] H. U. von Balthasar, *Thérèse of Lisieux: Story of a Mission* (London: Sheed and Ward, 1953).

[33] Balthasar, "Charis and charism", p. 309.

Church—as distinct from the way the Church is creatively affected in innovatory ways by the Holy Spirit in different places, at different times.

The Church is fundamentally constituted in her basic ongoing life, then, by the interplay of the Petrine, Johannine, and Marian factors, seen now not so much as contributions to the archetypal Christian experience (that is, the subjective perspective on ecclesiology), but as structuring principles in the Church's make-up.

The *Petrine* principle (as understood in this new context of reflection) is fairly obvious. Peter is given a share in the divine-human authority of Christ in the Church. His office of pastoral rule—a preeminent example of the activity of judging for which Jesus commissions the Twelve as a whole —will serve as the underlying rock for the Church's stability and unity. Humiliated by his own failures and by hard words from Jesus, the office laid on Peter at the Resurrection—in Balthasar's words, he will "pasture the flock of the incomparable Shepherd"[34]—is an utterly excessive demand, but what seems impossible is granted by the grace of Christ. This office is continued in the Church by the pope, though the Petrine principle is wider than simply the Petrine office and consists in the entire element of office-holding, official authority, in the Church.

Balthasar reminds his readers, if reminder be needed, that Protestants and the Orthodox are sceptical about the claims of the Roman bishop (the entire problematic of Tillard's later ecclesiology in a nutshell). Balthasar replies: if, among the constellation of people who surrounded Jesus and contributed intimately to his mission there is only one indi-

[34] Balthasar, *Office of Peter and the Structure of the Church*, p. 153.

vidual figure who has any kind of later embodiment in the Church (i.e., Peter), that figure will naturally look remarkably isolated in this regard, and doubts will inevitably arise as to whether Catholics have this right.

It is a false problem, for Peter is not alone in this regard. Next there is John. In the course of the Resurrection appearances in the Fourth Gospel, Jesus says to Peter about the Beloved Disciple, "If it is my will that he remain until I come, what is that to you?" (21:22). "This deliberately puzzling dictum has two facets: that the Beloved Disciple will really remain, for all times, in the Church, his presence not ceasing with his death; and that this presence, sealed by the will of the Lord of the Church, is exempt from Peter's control."[35] In the continuing life of the Church, the *Johannine* principle is the principle of "holy love", a love that accepts Peter's preeminence but also knows that it is itself the "Beloved". Holy Love—John—remains in the persons of the saints at Peter's side, at the side of the Church of office, so as to draw attention to the presence of the Lord, or perhaps to mediate between the Lord and Peter (one might think here of the role of Saint Bridget of Sweden and Saint Catherine of Siena vis-à-vis the last of the Avignon popes).

In their interrelation, love and office constitute a "huge, subtly complex fugue in the Church".[36] The Church in her unity is a communion in faith and love, and this might seem exclusively Johannine. But the Letters of Ignatius of Antioch show how the communion concerned is manifested in the official bond of the faithful with their bishop, while in the writings of Cyprian of Carthage, it is guarded by the

[35] Ibid., p. 160.
[36] Ibid.

unity of the bishops with each other, a unity embodied in the bishop of Rome. These Ignatian and Cyprianic considerations are undeniably Petrine in Balthasar's use of that term. He stresses, however, that just as the distinction between the Petrine and Johannine principles is subordinate to their complementary operation (in the kind of ways these patristic texts indicate), so likewise that distinction must not be taken to mean that officeholders in the Church can leave holy love to someone else. Precisely as vicars of Christ the Shepherd, Peter-figures are required to internalize the love John represents. (As illustration of these two interrelated points, one might suggest the collaboration of Blessed Teresa of Calcutta and Blessed John Paul II.)

But here is where we come to the *Marian* principle in the structure of the Church. In the following passage, the Irish Balthasarian scholar Brendan Leahy *names* the Petrine element first, but he *portrays* the Marian dimension in Balthasar's ecclesiology as always both subjacent and architectonic. In a sustaining manner, it undergirds the Petrine principle (it is "subjacent") and in an encompassing fashion, it is above and beyond it (it is architectonic):

> This sacrament of unity [the Church] contains both the exterior Petrine unity and the interior Marian unity. The Petrine unity is the hierarchical principle in the Church, the Marian element in the Church is Mary's spousal-maternal presence providing a Marian unity at the core of the earthly-heavenly Church, where the order of nature is fulfilled in grace, eros in agape, the created cosmos in ecclesial love.[37]

[37] B. Leahy, *The Marian Profile in the Ecclesiology of Hans Urs von Balthasar* (London: New City, 2000), p. 36.

Thanks to this Marian element—at once core within and sheltering canopy above—the Church is neither primarily bureaucratic nor chiefly to be investigated (demythologized? deconstructed?) by the efforts of sociologists. In Balthasar's eyes, conservative authoritarianism and radical chic walk hand in hand along the wrong path.

The Church's nature is to be Bride and Mother (de Lubac would agree!), specifically in her relation to the mystery of the Father, the communion of the Son, and the mission of the Holy Spirit. As those Trinitarian references indicate, this is not Mariology pathologically inflated, suffering from gigantism, invading ecclesiology's space. Rather, when the Church is considered as Christ's vis-à-vis, his Covenant partner, the Church the triune God gave mankind has a Marian heart. The complete scenario of revelation requires us to hold together in Christian doctrine these two vital areas— the Woman who responded and the Church that today and forever lives from her response.

There is far more to the Church than even the sacramental institution—more mystically, more charismatically, more cosmically. (We could see here if we wished a corrective to Tillard's vision.) The name of that "far more", so Balthasar would contend, is, by the grace of God in Christ, the name of Mary.

Balthasar, then, considers the Church in close relation to the Mother of God. His ecclesiology and his Mariology do not so much stand side by side as interweave. In Chapter 2 of this study, when speaking of the mark of holiness, I already had occasion to mention his joint effort with Joseph Ratzinger to point people to our Lady as the "primal Church". That effort was not confined to that significant collaboration. In his theological dramatics, he had this to say: "The Church has her origin in Mary, who is prior to all community and institution; only once the latter have come on the scene can Mary be described as an (eminent) member [simply] of the Church."[38]

The Marian principle is more foundational than the Petrine because it renders the Church in an all-embracing way holy and immaculate—enabling the mark of holiness identified by the Creed. This can only be a Marian *principle*, however, since only in the Mother of God is the Church already without stain or blemish or any such thing (though at the Eschaton, things—as Bouyer pointed out—will be different). The holiness of the Church is at present concretely constituted in Mary. That is how, in earthed reality (in her Assumption, Mary's body forms part of a new earth in living continuity with the old) the Church comes to have what Maritain termed (again, in Chapter 2) an indefectibly holy personality distinct from her all-too deficient personnel.

When the Church is born on the Cross, originating in the kenosis of the Son, the New Covenant made in his Blood is not sealed till the Daughter of Zion, waiting with the Beloved Disciple at the Cross' foot, has given her Yes to it, renewing thereby the *fiat* she gave to the entire saving economy at the Annunciation. The Church is more primordially feminine than she is masculine because she is more fundamentally Marian than she is Petrine. "The Marian *fiat*, unequalled in its perfection, is the all-inclusive protective and directive form of all ecclesial life. It is the interior form of *communio*."[39] Peter too must follow the Marian path and echo the fiat of the Mother of the Lord.

This of course is Balthasar's explanation of why the

[38] H. U. von Balthasar, *Theo-drama: Theological Dramatic Theory*, vol. 3: *Dramatis Personae: Persons in Christ* (San Francisco: Ignatius:, 1992), p. 452.
[39] Balthasar, *Glory of the Lord*, 1:208.

Church is a "she".[40] He does not apologise for proposing theologically a way to limit appropriately one ultra-Catholic element in his picture of the Church, his account of the Petrine principle, by invoking another that is just as ultra-Catholic, the Marian principle. (But he ironises that the ecclesial communities that derive from the sixteenth-century Reformation may regard this as casting out the Devil by means of Beelzebul, the prince of demons.)[41]

In this regard, Balthasar's ecclesiology corrects that of de Lubac, for whom, as we saw, the hierarchy embodies the motherhood of the Church. For Balthasar, the paternal (masculine) ordained ministry is, rather, anchored in the sphere of a maternity (a femininity) that characterizes the Church as a whole—and not any one "condition" or "rank" within it. The fading of the image of Mother Church from Catholic consciousness in the postconciliar period was for Balthasar, writing in the 1970s, an ecclesiological disaster waiting to happen. He thought it would lead, unless halted and reversed, to an increasingly soulless and ugly image of the Church, a countertraditional demand for the ordination of women and thus the subverting of the Christological symbolism of ministerial priesthood, and an evermore impersonal church of administrators (what he called *Ecclesia photocopians*) from which both women and men would flee in droves.

Balthasar left, then, a "constellational ecclesiology", in which much of what he has to say proceeds by way of reflection on a constellation of figures whose relations with Jesus Christ are constitutive of the human prolongation of his divine mission. The Gospel picture is isomorphic with

---

[40] Balthasar, "Who Is the Church?" in *Explorations in Theology*, vol. 2: *Spouse of the Word*, pp. 143–91.

[41] Balthasar, *Office of Peter and the Structure of the Church*, p. 184.

the portrait of later times, which is what we should expect if Catholic Christianity is the Church the apostles left behind.

A Conclusion on a Trio of Masters

Here we have certainly come a long way from a relatively straightforward account of the Church in terms of her marks such as I offered in the first half of this book.[42] But it was precisely so as to widen our conceptual (and imagistic) view that I decided to interrogate some masters as well. De Lubac on the Church as mystery and society, sacrament, and Mother; Tillard on the Church as a church of churches, defined from the starting point of the Eucharistic life: these too are amplifications of our view as generous as Balthasar's, if also less original and surprising.

For my final master, I turn, however, to a more conventional theological figure for whom the marks are key— even if, in his view, the view of a thoroughgoing Christian Scholastic, so likewise are her causes. And this is no accident. We cannot always be conceiving and imagining the Church in rare and audacious ways. We must also have, in the symphonic music of Catholic ecclesiology, a quiet *basso sostenuto*.

---

[42] But, apart from the essay "The Claim to Catholicity", which ranges far beyond ecclesiology, notice in Balthasar's last writing, a set of meditations on the Apostles' Creed, a little account of the marks of holiness, which he ascribes (unsurprisingly) to the Church's relation with the Virgin, and catholicity, where at the end of his life he now *combines* the qualitative and quantitative senses of the word—it is because she "shelters" the whole truth of God within her that the Church is called to communicate it to the nations. Thus H. U. von Balthasar, *Credo: Meditationen zum Apostolischen Glaubensbekenntnis*, 2nd ed. (Freiburg: Herder, 1990), p. 71.

8

CHARLES JOURNET

Journet's Life and Writing

Charles Journet was born near Geneva in 1891. He is, accordingly, the only one of our quartet to have been born in the nineteenth century, though he lived long enough to be made a cardinal towards the end of the pontificate of Paul VI, in 1975.[1] His formation was entirely Swiss, though not altogether of *La Suisse romande*: some of his education was done in the German-speaking canton, Schwyz, which borders the Lake of Lucerne, that same "Lake of the Four Forest Cantons" (*Vierwaldstättersee*) Balthasar could see from his family home.

Throughout his adult life, Journet was associated with the diocesan seminary of Fribourg, a cantonal capital often referred to as the "Little Rome". He was professor of dogmatics there from 1924 to 1970, and for most of that time editor of the journal *Nova et Vetera*, which he founded in 1926. (That must not be confused with its American homonym, founded in 2003; though inspired by Journet's work, it is quite distinct from the French-language publication.)

While Journet was principally a theologian of the Church,

---

[1] See for his life, G. Boissard, *Charles Journet, 1891–1975* (Paris: Salvator, 2008).

a specialist in ecclesiology (including the Church's relations with civil society),[2] he also wrote on what would now be called "fundamental theology"—both introducing the discipline[3] and studying the nature of revelation, dogma, and the character of our knowledge of God.[4] He explored such particular doctrinal themes as theodicy, Mariology, and the theology of the Mass,[5] and contributed to discussion of inner-Christian ecumenism and Christian-Jewish dialogue.[6] Intellectually, he positioned himself in close proximity to the French Thomist revival, and was friendly with not only its main lay stalwarts, Jacques Maritain and Étienne Gilson, but with the French Dominicans as well. He worked as a member of the theological commission that prepared for the Second Vatican Council, and at the Council's close in 1965 he was raised to the episcopate as a titular archbishop by Paul VI and named a cardinal. He died at his beloved Fribourg in the spring of 1975.

---

[2] C. Journet, *La juridiction de l'Eglise sur la cité* (Paris: Desclée de Brouwer, 1931); C. Journet, *Exigences chrétiennes en politique* (Paris: Desclée de Brouwer, 1945).

[3] C. Journet, *Introduction à la théologie* (Paris: Desclée de Brouwer, 1947).

[4] C. Journet, *Le Message révélé, sa transmission, son développement, ses dépendences* (Paris: Desclée de Brouwer, 1963); C. Journet, *Le Dogme, chemin de la foi* (Evreux: Fayard, 1963); *Connaissance et inconnaissance de Dieu* (Paris: Desclée de Brouwer, 1943).

[5] C. Journet, *Le Mal: Essai théologique* (Bruges: Desclée de Brouwer, 1961); Journet, *Esquisse du développement du dogme marial* (Paris: Alsatia, 1954); Journet, *La Messe, présence du sacrifice de la Croix* (Paris: Desclée de Brouwer, 1957).

[6] C. Journet, *Primauté de Pierre dans la perspective protestante et dans la perspective catholique* (Paris: Alsatia, 1963); Journet, *Destinées d'Israel: A propos de "salut par les juifs"* (Paris: Egloff, 1945).

Journet's "Church of the Word Incarnate": *Its Shape and Method*

Among Journet's ecclesiological writings, the masterwork is *The Church of the Word Incarnate*, whose initial book, subtitled *The Apostolic Hierarchy*, was published at Paris in 1941.[7] That first volume provides something of an overview of the entire work to come but deals more specifically with the note of apostolicity. A mere 734 pages (though a revised and augmented edition in 1955 brought that number up to 770), it was vastly eclipsed in size by the companion second volume, from 1951, on the Church's *Internal Structure and Catholic Unity*, which reached a grand total of 1,393 sides.[8] Journet had not really intended to be so cruel to his readers: the publishers bound together in one unwieldy volume books two and three of the overall work. The topic of the two, as the common subtitle indicates, was the Church's *Internal Structure and Catholic Unity*—unity and catholicity, then, conceived in close connexion the one with the other. A final volume, subtitled *An Essay on the Theology of Salvation History*, and concerned, in 724 pages, with the Church's historical preparation and her eschatological consummation, saw the light of day in 1969.[9]

It subsequently transpired that this latter material was really intended for book *five* (and hence the fourth volume) of the overall project. A posthumous supplement to the whole,

[7] C. Journet, *L'Eglise du Verbe incarné: Essai de théologie speculative*, vol. 1: *La Hiérarchie apostolique* (Paris: Desclée de Brouwer, 1941).

[8] C. Journet, *L'Eglise du Verbe incarné: Essai de théologie speculative*, vol. 2: *Sa structure interne et son unité catholique* (Paris: Desclée de Brouwer, 1951).

[9] C. Journet, *L'Eglise du Verbe incarné: Essai de théologie speculative*, vol. 3: *Essai de théologie de l'histoire de salut* (Paris: Desclée de Brouwer, 1969).

introduced by the theologian of the pontifical household, Georges Cottier, and published in 1999, turned out to constitute fragments (some 311 pages) of a never completed book *four* (and thus prospective volume three) on the holiness of the Church, with notable reference to the question of how the Church can be both holy yet composed of sinners—a crucial issue, as we have seen, in any approach to the second of her notes in the Great Creed.[10]

The first book of the magnum opus on the Church found an English translator,[11] but, overwhelmed perhaps by the task of translating the mammoth second volume, the project petered out. In 2004, however, the translation of an abridged version of the first and second volumes together, originally produced in French in 1958, appeared at San Francisco.[12]

So much for the literary history of *The Church of the Word Incarnate*, which explains its not entirely satisfactory shape. But what of Journet's method in this gigantic work? The cue lies in the phrase that extends its title in each of its volumes: *An Essay in Speculative Theology*. In a later generation, when approaches to the Church were often either more empirical and sociological, as in liberation theology (or the wider political theology), or, alternatively, more historical and thus concerned with relevant data from biblical and patristic texts, as with, say, Congar or Tillard, or, again, in one or another way synthetic, as with de Lubac and Balthasar,

---

[10] C. Journet, *L'Eglise sainte, mais non sans les pécheurs: Compléments inédits à "L'Eglise du Verbe incarné; La cause finale et la sainteté de l'Eglise"* (Saint Maur: Parole et Silence, 1999).

[11] C. Journet, *The Church of the Word Incarnate: An Essay in Speculative Theology* (London: Sheed and Ward, 1955).

[12] C. Journet, *Théologie de l'Eglise* (Paris: Desclée de Brouwer, 1958; 2nd ed.: 1960); *Theology of the Church* (San Francisco: Ignatius Press, 2004).

the notion that ecclesiology should be *primarily speculative* would seem surprising.

It is true that the word *speculative* can be used simply by way of distinction from *practical*, and so mean no more than "theoretical". But what Journet flagged up by using the word *speculative* was his plan for an ecclesiology that would present the being of the Church in terms of the sort of analysis typical of Christian Scholasticism, especially in its Thomistic guise. Journet sought to describe the Church in terms of four "causes": material, efficient, formal (or "exemplary"), and final, and this was a commonplace in such Neo-Scholastic tractates as the treatises on grace or the sacraments. He asks, then: What is the Church composed of? What makes her to be what she is? What kind of reality is she? And what is her purpose and goal?

Before Journet, the "method" shaped by the "four causes" was not so commonly found in ecclesiology, not, at any rate, in a comprehensive way. To those who think this sort of Aristotelian analysis of the reality of things illuminating, Journet's scheme seemed attractive. The opposite reaction could be expected from those who will find it too much of a conceptual straitjacket. In this study, as elsewhere in his corpus, Journet is a great lover of distinctions. His prose is elegant but not, generally speaking, poetic, though, owing to his profound immersion in the world of Western mysticism, it has moments of highly charged intensity. Taken overall, it is exceptionally clear. The combination of mystical resonance with conceptual clarity explains why so many of Journet's writings continue to be reprinted—as well as gathered together in a splendid overall edition, the *Oeuvres complètes*.[13]

---

[13] Begun with Editions Saint-Augustin (Saint Maurice) and continued by

Kinds of "Cause" of the Church

The first volume of *The Church of the Word Incarnate* deals with the Church's efficient cause, answering the question: What makes her what she is? To be more precise, Journet's opening volume takes as its principal theme that subordinate efficient cause of the Church which is the ministerial apostolic succession—or, in Journet's usage, "the hierarchy".

Naturally, Journet is well aware that the Church has more primordial efficient causes than merely the hierarchy. The question *What makes her what she is?* cannot possibly be answered without reference to the saving humanity of Jesus Christ, and, with, in, and behind that humanity, the action of the triune God himself. But so all-important is God in Christ in figuring out the Church that the problem Journet faced here was *embarrass de richesse*. Christ as man and the triune God have got to be, where the Church is concerned, far more than efficient causes.

For Christ as man is the Church's *exemplary* cause, and he is also her *final* cause. So much is implied—at any rate to the mind of a Christian Aristotelian—when the New Testament Letters call Jesus Christ the Church's "Head" and "Bridegroom". He is her Head because he is her exemplar, her pattern or template (her formal or exemplary cause); he is also her Bridegroom because he is her beloved goal, her much-desired end (her final cause).

Again, still speaking of the triune Lord of the Church, the Holy Spirit can scarcely be named as simply a primary *effi-*

---

the Parisian publishing house, Lethellieux. To avoid confusion, it is worth noting that in the *Oeuvres complètes*, the second volume of *L'Eglise du Verbe incarné* was split up into its originally intended two books, whereupon the third volume, as first published, becomes volume four, and the posthumous supplement, volume five. This edition will not, however, be cited in my text.

cient cause of the Church. He is far more than that. In Journet's words, the Holy Spirit amounts to her "personality, guest and soul".[14] Owing to its intimacy, such indwelling of the Spirit goes well beyond the range of any purely efficient causality. In his account of the Spirit's Indwelling in the Church, Journet was influenced by the Greek patristic tradition, and notably by Saint Cyril of Alexandria, who noted in the course of his magnificent *Commentary on the Gospel of John*:

> Certainly the holy prophets received in abundance the enlightenment and illumination of the Spirit, capable of instructing them in the knowledge of future things and in the understanding of mysteries, nevertheless we confess that in the faithful of Christ there is not only illumination but also the very dwelling and abode of the Spirit.[15]

For Journet, the Holy Spirit is the Church's Guest by taking up the love exhibited by her members and transforming it by the charity that he is—just as in the Kingdom he will transform their understanding by the Beatific Vision.

These topics are more fully addressed in the vast second volume of *L'Eglise du Verbe incarné*, where Journet, in the course of pursuing her marks of unity and catholicity, will seek to bring out more fully the character of the Church's dependence on both the humanity of Christ and the triune God himself.

Meanwhile, however, while introducing the topic of the Church by way of that lowliest of her efficient causes, the apostolic hierarchy, some distinctions are in order, and this is a Journet speciality. In volume two of his work, Journet

---

[14] Journet, *Church of the Word Incarnate*, p. 45.
[15] Cyril of Alexandria, *In Joannem* 5, at *Patrologia Graeca* 73, col. 757, cited in Journet, *Theology of the Church*, p. 82.

will be giving an account of Christ as not only exemplary and final cause of the Church, but also as her efficient cause in a more primordial sense than could ever be attached to the apostles or their successors. It is a sense of efficient cause which transcends that whereby the apostolic ministry is both such a cause and yet is subordinate to the greater causal effectiveness of the action of the divine Trinity. So here, at the opening of his project, and prior to outlining the four causes, Journet rightly flags up the difference between the impact of the Saviour and that of his envoys, the apostles and their successors.

The Fourfold Analysis

When we think of the Church as the ordained ministry taken together with the faithful they lead and serve, we shall ask, firstly, in this Aristotelian schema, what can be the Church's *material* cause? What is she "composed of"? The answer comes pat: human nature, as found in both hierarchs and faithful.

But then secondly, what is her *efficient* cause? What makes her to be what she is? Here the response must be a good deal more careful. As we have already had occasion to register, she has more than one. So far as efficient causes *beyond her own being* are concerned, they are God himself, the Church's primordial efficient cause, and the humanity of Christ, the instrumental efficient cause by which the Trinity's primary causality is in act in her regard—and can be so since the hypostatic union conjoins our Lord's humanity (the "instrument") to the Godhead. But the Church also has efficient causes that are at work *within the realm of her own being*.

The first of these which should be mentioned are the

powers of the apostolic hierarchy, powers used by Christ as a "separated instrument" so as to communicate to the Church the two modes of her priesthood: *the royal and universal priesthood of the faithful*—which the ordained confer, by the Redeemer's power, through the sacramental characters of Baptism and Confirmation, and *the ministerial priesthood of the ordained* themselves—which the bishops bestow, in the name of the Saviour, through the sacramental character of Order.

In Journet's ecclesiology, sacramental character—the abiding covenanted quality left in the soul by Baptism, Confirmation, Orders—is exceedingly important. It is the bestowal of character that makes the entire Church a liturgical mystery, in the praise and petition offered to the Father in union with the sacrificed Lamb. In the abridgment of the opening volumes of his ecclesiology, *Théologie de l'Eglise*, Journet sets out succinctly his understanding of sacramental character, and in the following words, explains how treating the Church as, via character, primarily a cultic, liturgical, or doxological reality, can be compatible with the Thomistic teaching that it is *charity* on which the perfection of all Christian existence turns:

> Just as Christ himself had been consecrated Priest by the Father in view of the [Paschal] sacrifice, so the three sacramental characters will consecrate the faithful, permitting them to participate, under diverse titles, in the grand Liturgy of which Christ is both the Priest and the Victim. Thanks to these sacramental characters, the Church with her priests and laity is totally priestly, totally engaged in the celebration of the mysterious worship that was consummated once for all on the Cross. It is true that all is perfected in love, not in worship, but Christian worship is the place of passage through which the double current

of love mounts from earth up to heaven and from heaven down to earth.[16]

The sacramental *characters*, along with the *graces* whose pledge they are, together with the *use* by persons, deploying their own freedom, of such characters and graces, should also count, then, as efficient causes that are set to work within the Church's own being, sustaining and prolonging it. These further causes dispose the Church's members, lay and ordained, to pursue the kinds of activity that are appropriate to her being and tend to procure the unity of action that befits her distinctive ontology.

But what is that distinctive ontology? Here we broach the question of the *formal* cause of the Church. What kind of reality *is* she? Journet takes as his guide to the formal intelligibility of the Church precisely a unity of action deriving from the operation of efficient causality in her regard. The combination of character, grace, and use makes her a sacramentally empowered community, whose charity is engaged supremely in worship yet not exclusively there, for it will be shaped by all the "lovingly interiorised" juridical directions—also described as "prophetic" impulses—furnished by the Church for Christian living.[17] He can thus identify the canonical or juridical side of things—pastoral measures put in place in the Church—with (of all things!) the prophetic voice of the Church because, in a very Thomistic way befitting this Dominican tertiary, Journet regards the goal of all pastoral work as *truth*, and thus it is that he subsumes the Church's prophetic or teaching office under her pastoral or ruling counterpart. It is through the distinctive unity of her active life—a life that is, in its highest reaches, a contemplative life, a life lived in conscious union with God

---

[16] Journet, *Theology of the Church*, p. 55.

[17] Journet, *L'Eglise du Verbe incarné*, 2:xxiii–xxiv.

—that what Journet calls "the soul of the Church" comes into play.

We saw how, in volume one of *The Church of the Word Incarnate*, Journet was willing to call the Holy Spirit in some sense the Church's "soul". He was indebted here both to Augustine, for whom what the soul is to the body the Holy Spirit is to the Body of Christ that is the Church,[18] and to Thomas, who echoes Augustine on this point in his *Commentary on the Apostles' Creed*. In volume two, more originally, Journet develops the idea that, as the Church's "uncreated Soul", the Spirit of the Father and the Son leaves in her by his activity a "created soul" (cf. Maritain's concept of "Church-personality", which I explained in Chapter 2). The Spirit's Indwelling is no mere resource awaiting the approach of individual members of the household of faith so as to be "touched and tasted" by them, as Journet, sure of his mystical sources, does not hesitate to say.[19] Rather, that Indwelling makes an impact, as the "Uncreated and Transcendent" leaves in its wake a principle of unity and life that is "created and inherent".[20] Theologically explicable in terms of the "capital grace" of the Word incarnate —the grace of Christ specifically as Head of the Church, the new Spirit-filled mankind—this "created soul" is best described, psychologically speaking, as a sort of ineradicable habit. It is a supernaturally empowered disposition, moving the Church's total membership in the direction of a love that Journet calls, in an idiom all his own, both "Christic and Christ-conforming".[21]

This habitual tendency is indefeasibly present in the Church

---

[18] Augustine, Sermon 267, 4.

[19] Journet, *L'Eglise du Verbe incarné*, 2:523.

[20] Journet sets out the case for this in ibid., pp. 565–79.

[21] E.g., at ibid., p. 634, where what is at issue is more specifically the role, in the economy of Spirit and Son, of the seven sacraments.

so that, if, *per improbabile*, all her members stumble at one and the same time, some at least will recover and rise again in exalted goodness. That provides the key for Journet's version of how to understand the way the Church can be in herself a holy Church—and yet contain sinners. The formal cause of the Church is a pneumatically and sacramentally originated charity, oriented to harmoniously coordinated Christocentric worship and action, and, thanks to this work of the Spirit in her, holiness will never be lacking to her.

A word further about such holiness seems appropriate in the context of the formal cause. The sanctity of the Church is, as the title suggests, the prevailing concern of Journet's posthumous *L'Eglise sainte, mais non sans les pécheurs*. But it is also crucial to appreciating the account of the "internal structure and catholic unity" of the Church set forth in the central volume of *L'Eglise du Verbe incarné* as published in his lifetime. "Catholic unity" meant for Journet the destiny of the Church to touch all men, both by incorporating them in her communion in their relation with eternal things and by illuminating their relation with temporal ones (in the sphere of civil society). And that could hardly be described, he thought, without reference to the order of charity—and hence the order of holiness. So Journet closes his account of the unity and catholicity of the Church in an excursus on "the Church 'without spot or wrinkle'" (a citation of Eph 5:27), where he catalogues the opinions on ecclesial holiness of a variety of authors—from the fourth-century archbishop of Constantinople John Chrysostom to the seventeenth-century French preacher and controversialist Jacques-Bénigne Bossuet[22]—and in this way looks ahead to a fuller treatment in the final volume left uncompleted at his death (on which more in a moment).

[22] Ibid., pp. 1115–28.

There remains the topic of the Church's *final* cause. What is her purpose and goal? Journet distinguishes between a goal that is transcendent vis-à-vis her being, and a goal that is immanent within that being. When we ask after her end in the *first*, transcendent, sense, it must be, supremely, God himself, considered as mankind's final *telos* and its sovereign good, and, in a secondary and instrumental yet indispensable way, Jesus Christ's humanity, considered as the duly furnished medium for attaining the "depths of God" (1 Cor 2:10, identified by Journet with the intimate life of the Holy Trinity),[23] and, as such, then, "the point of concentration of all the faithful".[24] We go to the triune God in the Church *through* the sacred humanity of our Lord, and in no other fashion.

When we go on to ask after the Church's end in the *second*, immanent, sense, Journet replies that it is the whole Church's "common good", and this consists in the happy way the efficient causes that sustain the Church's soul dispose her members to act in view of the transcendent end that is set before her. The soul of the Church, considered as the source of her unity, always finds expression in the visible communion of her life on earth, and in this manner is the enduring source of the catholicity of the Church's body. But that same soul finds its *perfect* expression when her members, drawing on her Christ- and Spirit-given resources, bring an appropriate quality of response to the divine call, and this they will do when they act by *charity* (that word again). Journet was as little willing as had been Thérèse of Lisieux, who influenced him here, to describe the essence of the Church without the mention of love.[25] It is from the

---

[23] Journet, *L' Eglise sainte*, p. 24.

[24] Journet, *Church of the Word Incarnate*, p. 47.

[25] G. Cottier, O.P., "Préface", in *L'Eglise sainte*, pp. v–vi. Cottier refers here to Journet's essay, "L'Eglise telle que la pense et la vit Thérèse de Lisieux",

Church's interior order conceived as an order of charity that her holiness proceeds, for, precisely when so conceived, the soul of the Church does not just unite her members, it also reflects the very holiness of God.[26]

And this is the heart of the posthumously collected fragments that make up *L'Eglise sainte*. The Church reflects the holiness of God in Jesus Christ by the way she prolongs the holy High Priesthood of our Mediator in the Mass and the other liturgical actions that surround the Eucharistic centre, by the way she prolongs his holy life in the states of life, the graces, and the virtues of her members, and by the way, too, she prolongs his holy message in her own teaching. She mirrors God's holiness insofar as *all of this tends towards perfect love*. And there is no (theological) possibility that such tending could fail altogether to meet the goal of charity. Were so dire an outcome to transpire, the Powers of the Underworld, contrary to the Saviour's promise, would have prevailed (cf. Mt 16:18).

Incidentally, it does not worry Journet that he has already described cultic, sacramental, and "oriented" charity as the *formal* cause of the Church, and now, in these unfinished remarks, treats it as her (immanent, rather than transcendent) *final* cause. Were not the Schoolmen content, he asks, to regard the soul, for instance, as at once efficient, formal, and final cause of the vivification of the body—so long as it was possible to discriminate the various senses or aspects in which the soul could be so described in those three distinct respects?[27] "Distinguish in order to unite" was not only a maxim of the philosophy of Jacques Maritain; it was also a principle of Journet's theology.

---

several times reprinted but most readily available in *Nova et Vetera* (Fribourg, 1975), pp. 300–308.

[26] Journet, *L'Eglise sainte*, p. 20.

[27] Journet, *L'Eglise du Verbe incarné*, p. 899.

The Many Names of the Church

Catholic theology, as Journet practised it, requires, though, not only conceptual analysis but also a language of mystical excess. In ecclesiology, Journet anticipated Congar—and hence the Second Vatican Council—in the multitude of names he lavished upon the Church. Though his preference is to speak of the Church under two titles, "The Mystical Body of Christ" and "The Place of Inhabitation (or Indwelling) of the Holy Spirit",[28] and he flags up this preference by speaking of these formulae as "major definitions",[29] he nevertheless lavishes upon her a plethora of names—Bride, plenitude (*plêrôma*), Kingdom of the Son of Man (or of God), tabernacle or house of God, temple of the Spirit—since by themselves the major definitions, though more far-reaching, by no means exhaust the Church's content.

Within this wider richness, the priority Journet accords the major definitions is not, however, arbitrary. Rather, it follows from his view, sustained through the various books of *L'Eglise du Verbe incarné*, that the missions of the Word and the Spirit are what enable—in ways clearly indicated by the formulae "Body of Christ" and "Inhabitation of the Spirit"—the Church's "created soul". Beginning at the Annunciation, the divine Trinity renders the Head and the Body one mystical person thanks to the humanity assumed by the Word in Mary, who is the Church's prototype and heart. Beginning at Pentecost, the divine Trinity comes to indwell the entire Body of the Church (thus constituted) through the inhabitation of the Holy Spirit. Hence no other concept or image of the Church can be more important than

---

[28] Journet, *L'Eglise du Verbe incarné*, 2:xi.
[29] Ibid., p. xxi.

these two. The created soul of the Church is brought into being "inasmuch as the grace of Christ the Head expands beyond itself, under the influence of the Holy Spirit, so as to make us participate in it",[30] and in this way to make possible—*pneumatically* possible—that cultic, sacramental, and "oriented" charity that Journet takes to be the formal cause of the "created soul" of the Church, whose efficient Cause is the Spirit's Indwelling in its relation to the capital grace of the Son. Here Journet's systematising impulse, more marked than that of Congar or, for that matter, any of the *nouvelle théologie* ecclesiologists I have considered in the second part of this study, renders him unwilling to leave a variety of concepts and images accumulating side by side. His resolve not to do so is very much part and parcel of his Thomistic inheritance.

Apostolicity as the (Pedagogically) Primary Note of the Church

For Journet, then, *Ecclesia* and *caritas*—when suitably understood in terms of a speculative analysis of Scripture in the light of theological tradition—amount to the same thing. I am sure it has been off-putting for Journet's potential English readership that, by contrast, the only translated volume of *L'Eglise du Verbe incarné* seems dominated by mitres and the tiara—concerns of Church hierarchy, which might appear at the antipodes from this "caritative" vision. It is, however, true that in Journet's ecclesiology as a whole, apostolicity can be described as the primary note of the Church, despite the fact that in the Creed it is mentioned last.

---

[30] Ibid., p. xxii.

The order of adjectives—one, holy, catholic, and apostolic—is for Journet, or so it would seem on a first hearing,
a crescendo, not a diminuendo. In an early article on the
note of apostolicity, while affirming the inseparability of all
four of the marks of the Church, he argued that, precisely
owing to that inseparability, if one can identify correctly one
note, then it will be possible to uncover the rest—which
are distinct from it conceptually, but not in the reality to
which they refer. And here apostolicity is the most helpful
way into the mystery, at least if we understand such apostolicity as "the power that gives birth to the Church".[31]
The way Journet explains this point enables us to see that
he is not proposing to rewrite the Creed by turning upside
down the sequence of the Church's notes (contrast my criticism of theological radicals on the Trinitarian ordering in
Chapter 1). Rather, he is approaching the matter in terms
of pedagogy. Apostolicity enjoys *pedagogical* primacy.

Apostolicity draws to our attention that particular efficient cause of the Church's being which is plainest to the
sympathetic investigator. And this is "a hierarchy invested
for all time with the power conferred on the Apostles by
Christ".[32] It belongs to divine wisdom that people should
need each other (here Journet cites the *Dialogue* of Saint
Catherine of Siena), not least in the work of redemption.
And yet the prominent place the apostles occupy in the
Church is not so much intended to exalt hierarchs as to
let God be God. The apostolic ministry, so far from making the Church man-centred, "marks the dependence of the
Church as found in all the faithful, of the Church, believing

---

[31] C. Journet, "L'apostolicité, propriété et note de la véritable Eglise", *Revue thomiste* 37 (1937): 167–200, here at p. 169. This essay would emerge,
retouched, as the tenth chapter of *L'Eglise du Verbe incarné*, vol. 1.

[32] Journet, *Church of the Word Incarnate*, p. 17, n. 1.

and loving, on its divine causes".[33] Via the holy apostles, the Church issues through the manhood of Christ from the triune Lord.

Still, the way Journet privileges the note of apostolicity does place great emphasis on the bearers of the apostolic ministry, and hence, for the contemporary Church, on pope and bishops, priests and deacons. But he is also very well aware of the limits to that ministry's scope. The hierarchy possesses seemingly opposed characteristics: for its proper purposes, it is perfect, yet it cries out for completion. It is at one and the same time universally effective and requiring continual supplementation.

> The apostolic ministry is "perfect" inasmuch as it alone confers those sanctifying effects which are to bring the Church militant to her perfect historical age, to her ultimate specific form, which are to make her the completed Body of Christ, the community having Christ for Head and Christians for members, the marvellous abode in which God dwells somewhat as He dwells in Christ Himself.[34]

But the hierarchy is also in dire need of supplementation by graces over and above what it can offer by its own (supernaturally derivative) agency. Graces are needed that stem from elsewhere than the Word and sacraments as confided to the care of these stewards—needed, firstly, if souls are to be prepared to receive what the apostolic hierarchy can give, and, secondly, if Christians are to perpetuate on a day-to-day basis what it is the apostolic mission can bestow. On both counts, a "continuous and secret influx" from the Mediator, Jesus Christ, is unconditionally necessary.[35]

[33] Ibid.
[34] Ibid., p. 12.
[35] Ibid.

What Journet has in mind is, on the one hand, the prevenient grace that prepares the way for our justification and the theological virtues of faith, hope, and charity that God infuses into us by way of sanctifying grace, and, on the other hand, the flow of charisms and the actual, or one-off, graces we receive at discrete moments in our lives. The charisms enable us to play our particular part in building up God's Kingdom. The actual graces help us to meet challenges—whether coming from inner temptations or from the outer environment—which we must if we are to live a Christian life at all worth the name.

The same dialectic—Yes, and No—accompanies (and qualifies) Journet's statement that the outreach of the hierarchy is universal. On the one hand, that claim is made explicit in the Great Commission given to the bearers of the apostolic ministry at the end of Saint Matthew's Gospel (28:19a–20). Its mission is "to extend to all nations and to endure for all time".[36] But can its contact with mankind really be universal in the proper sense? Yes, it can.

> First of all, de jure, because the hierarchy is the unique visible instrument chosen by God to form His Church here below and communicate the fullness of grace and evangelical truth to the world; and de facto as well, for on the day of Pentecost the hierarchy established contact with a multitude of men of all conditions, classes and tongues.[37]

But does that mean, then, that before (or by the time of) the Parousia the action of the hierarchy will have come to affect by direct contact all men, both in their corporate solidarities and as individuals? Well no, that can scarcely be

[36] Ibid.
[37] Ibid., pp. 12–13.

presumed. And yet the will of God is the salvation of all. So Journet concludes that while

> only the outpouring of grace that comes of visible contact with the hierarchy will enable the Church to attain to its final specific state and grow to the fullness of the body of Christ in this world . . . , this outpouring, though plenary and *universal* in its order, calls for another [outpouring], altogether spiritual and effected from a distance; an outpouring whose normal purpose it will be to complete the former, but whose extraordinary purpose it will also be in a certain measure to supply for it.[38]

So there is a realism and sobriety here after all.

Ecclesial and Non-ecclesial People

Despite the importance for his ecclesiology of the ordained ministry (inevitable in any Catholic writer), and, more widely, his frequent recurrence to the categories of not only dogmatic theology but also canon law (in which only Tillard, among the authors represented here, really follows him), Journet's mind continually turned towards the question of the unevangelised: those who are not incorporated, by faith and Baptism, into the visible Church and who know neither her teaching nor the shape of her common life. In the final volume of his master work, he would situate the Church within the entirety of salvation history between creation and Parousia, where these vast swathes of ecclesially untutored humanity become apparent.[39]

Yet he finds it entirely possible to present this wider picture in relation to each of the two "powers"—order (the

---

[38] Ibid., p. 13; italics are original.

[39] Journet, *L'Eglise du Verbe incarné*, vol. 3, a work which does not boast in vain its subtitle, *Essai de théologie de l'histoire de salut*.

priestly function) and jurisdiction (the pastoral function)—
by which, on his account, the offices of Christ the Redeemer
resonate in the Church through the time since Pentecost.
Reflecting on each of these powers brings with it, he finds,
a message of consolation for the unchurched.

The visible cultus to which the Church's priestly office is
directed is offered first and foremost for those who "belong
visibly and completely to the Church"—but not exclusively
for them, unconscious of its celebration though they may
be.[40] Since the Church's worship, and above all the Mass,
brings us the presence of the Mediator "who gave himself
as a ransom for all" (1 Tim 2:6), that worship is also offered
for those who belong to her "invisibly and incompletely",[41]
and this means, *so far as the world is concerned*, those who belong to her not at all.

What, then, in this perspective, is the difference between
ecclesial and non-ecclesial people? Believers, who are in full
communion with the Church have a salvific responsibility
for others, whereas those who, unwittingly, are merely in
receipt through the Church's intercession of Christ's saving influence have no such obligations. It is harder to be a
member of the Church than to forego the burden of that
privilege. As Kingdom-bearers, our lives are no longer our
own.

And just as the Church in her prayer and worship touches
those beyond her visible bounds by the power of *order*, so
likewise it is with the power of *jurisdiction*, with its mission
of shepherding people through the annunciation of *veritas*,
the divine truth. Journet wrote:

It would be gravely erroneous to think that the directions
of the jurisdictional power are content to act on the world

---

[40] Journet, *Church of the Word Incarnate*, p. 60.
[41] Ibid.

only directly, and only at the point where they are openly and visibly received. In manifesting divine truth with unique power, they make their influence felt far beyond these limits. They attain, by repercussion, to much wider circles. They help to enlighten, sustain and save many of those who, without being in the Church openly, fully, in achieved act, belong to her already hiddenly, imperfectly, in initial act. And the more the cultural unification of races and peoples progresses, so much the more does spiritual influence and jurisdiction tend to overflow and to pass far beyond the apparent and humanly discernible limits of the Church.[42]

One might think in this connexion of a number of the modern popes, occupants of Peter's chair of teaching, who have sought to reach out to the unchurched not only by direct evangelization but also in pursuit of those truths, whether metaphysical or moral, that are in the Church's possession yet can also be affirmed on other grounds (maybe one should say, rather, "intuited" or "surmised"). The social doctrine of the Church, in its entire trajectory from Leo XIII to Benedict XVI and presented by them as a remedy for the ills of the contemporary socio-economic order, exemplifies the kind of thing Journet has in mind. So does, in a further example, the appeal for a rediscovery of a sapiential metaphysics, a real philosophical wisdom, in the encyclical *Fides et ratio* of Pope John Paul II.

A Marian Conclusion

But actually for Journet, the last word should really be reserved not for Peter (in his vicars) but for Mary (in herself, which is as much as to say, in her symbiotic relation with

---

[42] Journet, *Church of the Word Incarnate*, p. 381.

the Church of her Son from which she is inseparable). It is by seeing the Church in Marian perspective, and seeing the Mother of the Lord in Christological perspective, that we can best understand how men beyond the manifest range of the *Catholica* may enter the ambit of salvation. The new Adam is never without the new Eve, who gave her *fiat* to both his incarnate existence and also (since the Incarnate One was essentially the Redeemer) his reconciling work, thus becoming, in an inverted recapitulation of Eve's disastrous role in the Garden, the helpmate of the Saviour. That *fiat* is now shared with the Church, which had as her primal member the "worthy Mother of a Saviour God",[43] who fulfilled her role in climactic fashion when she became the Woman at the Cross. Here the two Swiss theologians I have presented, Journet and Balthasar, are at one.

> In Mary the Church becomes co-redemptory [*sic*] namely, of all men, whether they know it or not. . . . The redemptive mediation of Christ carries the universal co-redemption of the Virgin, who in turn carries the corporate coredemptive mediation of the Church and the particular co-redemptive mediations of Christians, for there are some souls that carry others, as a planet its moons.[44]

Just so Saint Monica, by a derivative mediation from Christ, "carried" her erring son, the amorous student, and subsequently Manichean "hearer", the still unbaptised Augustine. This is a high doctrine of coredemption which will seem alien, no doubt, to many Protestant readers of this book, should they come across it. But really such doctrine is based on something very simple that every Evangelical will recognize: in the Lord Jesus Christ we can pray for each other. Only we must add with the Scholastics, that the

---

[43] Journet, *L'Eglise du Verbe incarné*, 2:382–453, here at p. 386.
[44] Journet, *Theology of the Church*, p. 94.

closer one is to a source (and here the source is the redeem-ing God-man), the more one participates in its effects.

Thus this Scholastic—or Neo-Scholastic—ecclesiology is not, after all, so lacking in imaginative *élan*. Journet stands alongside not only Balthasar but de Lubac in stressing the Marian character of the Church. And if we have to look hard for the same insight in Tillard, it remains the case that, in any celebration of the "authentic Eucharist" in the churches of both East and West, the figure of the *Theotokos*, the *Madonna*, otherwise known as the Mother of the Lord, will never be far from the altar-table.

> The Virgin is in the Church. She is, within the Church, the place towards which the Church, in her other mem-bers, tends ceaselessly to draw near, as the curve to its asymptotic goal and the polygon towards the circle.[45]

> When we say that the Church is Marian, we wish to sig-nify that Mary is interiorized in the Church, to which she communicates her spirit.[46]

---

[45] Journet, *L'Eglise du Verbe incarné*, 2:393.
[46] Ibid., p. 428.

CONCLUSION:
SHOULD WE LOVE THE CHURCH?

This title of a Balthasar essay on ecclesiology is unexpected
—and yet who could declare it nonpertinent?[1] The Swiss
divine points out that no command to love the Church is
found in the New Testament, where the mandate given us
favours only God and our neighbour. And yet, as Balthasar
also remarks, if the imitation of Christ is to signify anything,
we can hardly ignore the message of the Letter to the Ephesians. Our Lord Jesus Christ himself "loved the Church
and gave himself up for her" so that she might be holy and
immaculate; that text (Eph 5:25–27) enters so unavoidably
into discussion when Catholic authors consider the second
of the Church's notes in the relevant clause of the Creed.
And indeed, any commentator who takes seriously the authority of the Bible must let this Scripture have its say.

We love the Church because Christ has loved her. We
love her because he has taken her as his Bride. And we also
love her, despite the failings, often grave and sometimes hor-
rendous, of her members, so that she may be, in the length
and breadth of her communion, that which she already is,
owing to his redemptive work, in her own indestructible
personality, which is the hidden fruit of his grace.

[1] H. U. von Balthasar, "Should We Love the Church?" in *Explorations in
Theology*, vol. 4: *Spirit and Institution* (San Francisco: Ignatius Press, 1995),
pp. 169–208.

It is because we love her, in a mimesis of the Lord's own love for his Bride, that we submit ourselves to work for the fullest realisation of her marks: not only the mark of holiness, which we enhance every time we emerge victorious in the spiritual warfare with the world, the flesh, and the Devil, but the others as well.

Every time I shape my understanding to the mould found in her dogmatic consciousness or submit myself to the authority of her forms of worship or seek to serve her members in practical ways, I intensify the mark of unity. Whenever I support her missionary activity, by whatever means, or try to bring the culture I have acquired or inherited into symbiotic relation with her life and faith, understanding the latter as fully as my resources will allow, I extend her catholicity. And if in showing others, in word or deed, how I value what has been transmitted to me, in Scripture and Tradition, from the apostles by, for example, kissing the ring— or, if I am a Catholic of the Eastern rites, the hand—of a bishop, I venerate the apostolic hierarchy which joins us in one direction to Pentecost and in another to the Parousia, then on those occasions I enlarge the scope of apostolicity in the Church.

This book has considered the four marks of the one, holy, catholic, and apostolic Church for their own sake. But it has also examined a quartet of ecclesiologies for the further light those masters can shed. We have seen with de Lubac how she is sacrament of Christ and Mother of Christians; with Tillard, how she is formed by the mysteries she celebrates; with Balthasar, how she is at once a Marian, a Petrine, and a Johannine Church, and a Church where, thanks to the Eastertide events, the Holy Spirit works both mystically and institutionally in the service of the economy of the Son. And with Journet, we have concluded that, if she is the Body of Christ and the dwelling-place of the Spirit, her real name is *caritas*. That is why the Madonna, the Mother of Fair Love, can be not only at her goal but at her heart.

SELECT BIBLIOGRAPHY

Auer, A. *The Church: The Universal Sacrament of Salvation*. Washington: Catholic University of America, 1993.

Bainvel, J. 'Apostolicité', *Dictionnaire de théologie catholique*. Vol. 1, fasc. 2, cols. 1618–1631. Paris: Letouzey & Ané, 1931.

Balthasar, H. U. von. *Bernanos: An Ecclesial Existence*. San Francisco: Ignatius Press, 1996.

————. *'Casta Meretrix'*. In *Explorations in Theology*. Vol. 2: *Spouse of the Word*, pp. 193–288. San Francisco: Ignatius Press, 1991.

————. 'The Claim to Catholicity', in *Explorations in Theology*. Vol. 4: *Spirit and Institution*, pp. 65–121. San Francisco: Ignatius Press, 1995.

————. *Explorations in Theology*. Vol. 2: *Spouse of the Word*. San Francisco: Ignatius Press, 1991. Vol. 4: *Spirit and Institution*. San Francisco: Ignatius Press, 1995.

————. *The Glory of the Lord: A Theological Aesthetics*. Vol. 1: *Seeing the Form*. San Francisco: Ignatius Press, 1982.

Where English translations are available, these titles are preferred for this bibliography, even if the original-language edition has been named, referred to, or quoted from, in the body of the text. Those who wish to make use of the original texts will have little difficulty in tracking their titles and publication details.

————. *In the Fullness of Faith: On the Centrality of the Distinctively Catholic.* San Francisco: Ignatius Press, 1988.

————. *Mysterium Paschale: The Mystery of Easter.* Edinburgh: T. & T. Clark, 1990.

————. *The Office of Peter and the Structure of the Church.* San Francisco: Ignatius Press, 1986.

————. "Should We Love the Church?" In *Explorations in Theology.* Vol. 4: *Spirit and Institution.* San Francisco: Ignatius Press, 1995, pp. 169–208.

————. *Theo-drama: Theological Dramatic Theory.* Vol. 3: *Dramatis Personae: Persons in Christ.* San Francisco: Ignatius Press, 1992.

————. *Theo-logic: Theological Logical Theory.* Vol. 3: *The Spirit of Truth.* San Francisco: Ignatius Press, 2005.

————. *The Theology of Henri de Lubac: An Overview.* San Francisco: Ignatius Press, 1991.

————. 'Who Is the Church?' In *Explorations in Theology.* Vol. 2: *Spouse of the Word.* San Francisco: Ignatius Press, 1991, pp. 143–92.

Balthasar, H. U. von, and J. Ratzinger. *Mary: The Church at the Source.* San Francisco: Ignatius Press, 2005.

Beinert, W. *Um das dritten Kirchenattribut: Die Katholizität der Kirche im Verständnis der evangelisch-lutherisch und römisch-katholischen Theologie der Gegenwart.* 2 vols. Essen: Ludgerus, 1964.

Biedermann, O.S.A., H. M. "Apostilizität als Gottes Gabe im Leben der Kirche". *Ostkirchliche Studien* 37 (1988): 38–54.

Boissard, G. *Charles Journet, 1891–1975.* Paris: Salvator, 2008.

Bouyer, L. *The Church of God: Body of Christ and Temple of the Holy Spirit.* Chicago: Franciscan Herald Press, 1982.

Bracken, J. A. 'Ecclesiology and the Problem of the One and the Many'. *Theological Studies* 43 (1982): 298–311.

Congar, Y. *L'Eglise une, sainte, catholique et apostolique.* Paris: Cerf, 1970.

Cottier, G. "Eglise sainte: L'Eglise sans péché, non sans pécheurs". *Nova et vetera* (Fribourg) 66, no. 4 (1991): 9–27.

Dewailly, L. M. "Note sur l'histoire de l'adjectif 'apostolique'". *Mélanges de science religieuse* (1948): 141–52.

Dulles, A. *The Catholicity of the Church.* Oxford: Clarendon, 1985.

———. "The Church as Communion". In *New Perspectives on Historical Theology: Essays in Memory of John Meyendorff,* pp. 125–39. Ed. B. Nassif. Grand Rapids, Mich., and Cambridge: Eerdmans, 1996.

———. 'The Church, the Churches and the Catholic Church'. *Theological Studies* 33 (1972): 179–234.

Famerée, J. "L'ecclésiologie du Père Yves Congar: Essai de synthèse critique". *Revue des Sciences Philosophiques et Théologiques* 76 (1992): 377–49.

———. "Orthodox Influence on the Roman Catholic Theologian Yves Congar, O.P.: A Sketch". *Saint Vladimir's Theological Quarterly* 39 (1995): 409–16.

Feckes, C. *Das Mysterium der heiligen Kirche: Dogmatische Untersuchungen zum Wesen der Kirche.* Paderborn: Schöningh, 1934.

Fontbona i Missé, J. *Comunión y sinodalidad: La ecclesiología eucarística después de N. Afanasiev en I. Zizioulas y J. M. R. Tillard.* Barcelona: Editorial Herder, 1994.

Garrigues, J. M., and M. J. Le Guillou. "Statut eschatologique et caractère ontologique de la succession apostolique". *Revue thomiste* 75 (1975): 395–427.

Hamer, J. "Le Saint-Esprit et la catholicité de l'Eglise". *Angelicum* 11 (1969): 387–410.

Hastings, A. *One and Apostolic.* London: Darton, Longman, and Todd, 1963.

Healy, N., and D. L. Schindler. "For the Life of the World: Hans Urs von Balthasar on the Church's Eucharist". *The Cambridge Companion to Hans Urs von Balthasar,* ed. E. T. Oakes, S.J., and D. Moss, pp. 51–63. Cambridge: Cambridge University Press, 2004.

Journet, C. *The Church of the Word Incarnate: An Essay in Speculative Theology.* London: Sheed and Ward, 1955.

———. *L'Eglise du Verbe incarné: Essai de théologie speculative.* Vol. 1: *La Hiérarchie apostolique.* 1941. 2nd ed., Paris: Desclée de Brouwer, 1955. Vol. 2: *Sa structure interne et son unité catholique.* Paris: Desclée de Brouwer, 1951. Vol. 3: *Essai de théologie de l'histoire de salut.* Paris: Desclée de Brouwer, 1969.

———. *L'Eglise sainte, mais non sans pécheurs: Compléments inédits de L'Eglise du Verbe incarné; La cause finale et la sainteté de l'Eglise.* Saint Maur: Parole et Silence, 1999.

———. "Note sur l'Eglise sans tache ni ride". *Revue thomiste* 49 (1949): 208–11.

———. *Theology of the Church.* San Francisco: Ignatius Press, 2004.

Kasper, W. "Die Einheit der Kirche nach dem II. Vatikanischen Konzil". *Catholica* 33 (1979): 262–77.

Kelly, J. N. D. " 'Catholic' and 'Apostolic' in the Early Centuries". *One in Christ* 6 (1970): 274–87.

Kirk, K. E., ed. *The Apostolic Ministry*. London: Hodder and Stoughton, 1946.

Lanne, E. "L'Eglise une". *Irénikon* 50 (1977): 46–58.

Leahy, B. *The Marian Profile in the Ecclesiology of Hans Urs von Balthasar*. London: New City, 2000.

Lubac, H. de. *At the Service of the Church: Henri de Lubac Reflects in the Circumstances That Occasioned His Writings*. San Francisco: Ignatius Press, 1993.

——. *Catholicism: Christ and the Common Destiny of Man*. San Francisco: Ignatius Press, 1988.

——. *The Christian Faith: An Essay on the Structure of the Apostles' Creed*. San Francisco: Ignatius Press, 1986.

——. *The Church: Paradox and Mystery*. Shannon, Ireland: Ecclesia Press, 1969.

——. *Corpus mysticum: The Eucharist and the Church in the Middle Ages*. Notre Dame, Ind.: University of Notre Dame Press, 2007.

——. *The Motherhood of the Church*. San Francisco: Ignatius Press, 1982.

——. *The Splendour of the Church*. London and New York: Sheed and Ward, 1956.

Michel, A. "La sainteté, note de l'Eglise". In *Dictionnaire de théologie catholique*. Vol. 14, fasc. 1, cols. 847–65. Paris: Letouzey & Ané, 1939.

————. 'L'unité de l'Eglise'. In *Dictionnaire de théologie catholique*. Vol. 15, fasc. 2, cols. 2172–230. Paris: Letouzey & Ané, 1950.

Möhler, J. A. *Unity in the Church, or the Principle of Catholicism Presented in the Spirit of the Church Fathers of the First Three Centuries*. Washington: Catholic University of America Press, 1996.

Moureau, H. "Catholicité". In *Dictionnaire de théologie catholique*. Vol. 2, fasc. 2, cols. 2000–2012. Paris: Letouzey & Ané, 1932.

Mühlen, H. *Una mystica Persona: Die Kirche als das Mysterium der Identität des Heiligen Geistes in Christus und den Christen: eine Person in vielen Personen*. 2nd ed. Paderborn: Aschendorf, 1967.

Nicolas, O.P., J. H. *Synthèse dogmatique: De la Trinité à la Trinité*. Fribourg: Editions universitaires de Fribourg, 1985.

Oakes, E. T. *Pattern of Redemption: The Theology of Hans Urs von Balthasar*. New York: Continuum, 1994.

O'Callaghan, P. "The Holiness of the Church in Early Christian Creeds". *Irish Theological Quarterly* 54 (1988): 59–65.

————. "The Holiness of the Church in *Lumen gentium*". *The Thomist* 52 (1988): 673–701.

Paul, D. "Sinners in the Holy Church: A Problem in the Ecclesiology of St Augustine". *Studia patristica* 9 (1966): 404–15.

Ruddy, C. *The Local Church: Tillard and the Future of Catholic Ecclesiology*. New York: Crossroad, 2006.

Saward, J. "Mary and Peter in the Christological Constellation: Balthasar's Ecclesiology". *The Analogy of Beauty:*

The Theology of Hans Urs von Balthasar, pp. 103–33. Ed. J. Riches. Edinburgh: T. & T. Clark, 1986.

———. *The Mysteries of March: Hans Urs von Balthasar on the Incarnation and Easter.* London: Collins, 1990.

Schindler, D. L., ed. *Hans Urs von Balthasar: His Life and Work.* San Francisco: Ignatius Press, 1991.

Schnackenburg, R. *The Church in the New Testament.* Freiburg and London: Herder & Herder, 1965.

Schnackers, H. *Kirche als Sakrament und Mutter: Zur Ekklesiologie von Henri de Lubac.* Frankfurt: Lang, 1979.

Sullivan, F. A. *The Church We Believe In: One, Holy, Catholic, and Apostolic.* Dublin: Gill & MacMillan, 1988.

Thils, G. *Les notes de l'Eglise dans l'apologétique catholique depuis la Réforme.* Gembloux: J. Duclot, 1937.

Tillard, J. M. R. *The Bishop of Rome.* London: SCM Press, 1983.

———. *Church of Churches: The Ecclesiology of Communion.* Collegeville, Minn.: Liturgical Press, 1992. In this case, the French original is definitely preferable: *Eglise d'églises: L'ecclésiologie de communion.* Paris: Cerf, 1987.

———. *L'Eglise locale: Ecclésiologie de communion et catholicité.* Paris: Cerf, 1995.

———. *L'Eucharistie, Pâques de l'Eglise.* Paris: Cerf, 1964.

———. *Flesh of the Church, Flesh of Christ: At the Source of the Ecclesiology of Communion.* Collegeville, Minn.: Liturgical Press, 2001.

Zizioulas, J. *Being as Communion: Studies in Personhood and the Church.* New York: St. Vladimir's Seminary Press, 1985.